MAIN LINE ENTERTAINS

Presented by The Saturday Club

MAIN LINE ENTERTAINS
Saturday Club Style

Library of Congress Control Number:
2005901778
ISBN: 0-9650818-2-6

Edited, Designed, and Manufactured by
Favorite Recipes® Press
An imprint of

P.O. Box 305142
Nashville, Tennessee 37230
800-358-0560

Art Director: *Steve Newman*
Book Design: *Brad Whitfield and Susan Breining*
Project Editor: *Linda Jones*

Manufactured in the United States of America
First Printing: 2005
15,000 copies

Additional copies of *Main Line Entertains* may be obtained by sending $29.95 each plus $4.50
to cover postage and handling (Pennsylvania residents, add $1.80 sales tax) to:
THE SATURDAY CLUB
Main Line Entertains Sales Department • 117 West Wayne Avenue • Wayne, Pennsylvania 19087

EXECUTIVE COOKBOOK COMMITTEE

Chairperson – *Lisa Smith*

Marketing and Sales – *Jennifer Newhall*

Sponsorship Coordinator – *Cindy Bevan-Wilson*

Recipe Collection Coordinator – *Lesley Blatchford*

Recipe Testing Coordinator – *Anne Bolton*

Photo Shoot Stylist – *Maureen Weaver*

Photo Shoot Coordinator – *Julie Beverly*

Photo Shoot Captains:

Colleen Comerford

Margaret Hondros

Vaughn Honigman

Sara Leyden

Laura Marino

Nancy Rainer-Wallace

Treasurer – *Barbara Miller*

CLUB MISSION

Founded in 1886, The Saturday Club originated as a forum for the education and cultural enrichment of women. Today, the Club's mission has expanded to include direct service and philanthropic support to charitable organizations in the Greater Philadelphia area. Additionally, the Club is committed to maintaining its turn-of-the-century Tudor-style clubhouse, which is listed on the National Register of Historic Places and is integral to the life of the membership and surrounding community.

OUR WONDERFUL SPONSORS

We could not have produced Main Line Entertains *without the generous support of our wonderful sponsors.*
On behalf of the Main Line Entertains *Cookbook Committee and The Saturday Club,*
thank you from the bottom of our plates!

CHAMPAGNE SPONSOR

Cortie Wetherill's Family of Dealerships:

BMW of the Main Line
MINI of the Main Line

Devon Hill Motors BMW & VW
Main Line BMW Motorcycles

SOMMELIER SPONSORS

Main Line Health
The Little House Shop &
The Little House Shop Stationers

Sand Castle Winery
Wachovia Wealth Management

CABERNET SPONSORS

Coventry Kitchens, Inc.
Hartstrings Childrenswear
Weichert Realtors, Hoey Group,
Avalon, NJ

Carl Schaedel and Co.
Walter J. Cook Jewelers
Weichert Realtors, Wayne, PA

CHARDONNAY SPONSORS

Ardmore Farmers Market
Carol DeYoung
Environments HC

P. J. Hollyhocks
Rita's Water Ice, Inc.
Valley Forge Flowers
Lancaster County Farmers Market

ZINFANDEL SPONSORS

Main Line Party Rentals
The Madison School of Etiquette and Protocol
Gatherings Food Source

MAJOR CONTRIBUTORS

Main Line Entertains is a collaboration of many individuals. We thank you for your generous contributions of time, talent, energy, and resources.

VALLEY FORGE FLOWERS, whose inspired arrangements will forever bloom in our pages.

CHEF VALERIE JAMISON, Food Stylist, a true culinary artist.

RICHARD W. GRETZINGER, Director of Photography, who guided our project through his creative lens.

WHOLE FOODS OF DEVON, for providing a well-stocked pantry.

ENVIRONMENTS HOME COUTURE, who so graciously gave of their time and energy to assist us in creating the "perfect environment."

SPECIAL THANKS

We thank you sincerely for your part in this endeavor. If we have inadvertently failed to include your name, please accept our apologies.

To the Main Line Chamber of Commerce, and especially to Robert Pucci, Chamber President, for believing in us and endorsing our book as the "Official Cookbook of the 21st-Century Main Line."

To the families and historic organizations who so graciously allowed us into their beautiful homes and landmarks for the photographs in this cookbook:

Ardmore Farmers Market
Ardrossan
Chanticleer
B. J. & Richard Johnson, Brooke Farm
Lancaster County Farmers Market
The Main Line Express: Rosemont, Haverford, Strafford, and Radnor

Dr. & Mrs. Donald J. Rosato, St. Matthews Place
Donald & Peggy Sheehy
Mr. & Mrs. Cortright Wetherill, Wide Rill Farm
Valley Forge National Historical Park
Private residents who wish to remain anonymous

To all of our wonderful spouses and families for their endless support and incredible endurance in making this project a reality. We love you!

For the success of our previous Main Line Classics Cookbooks:

Main Line Classics, Introduced 1982
Main Line Classics II: Cooking Up A Little History, Introduced 1996

TRIBUTES

The following members of The Saturday Club honor their friends and family, who have inspired them to find enrichment, joy, and love in all that they do.

Thank you, **Mom**, for more than thirty-seven years of great cooking memories! You are the best cook I know! I love you! **Lisa Smith**

To the **Callahan, Hammett,** and **Newhall Families**, the love, traditions, and memories we share are some of my most important treasures. With all my love, **Jennifer Newhall**

Christine Kozeracki thanks her mother, **Theresa Higgins**, for being her constant inspiration and for teaching her daughters and granddaughters to appreciate their own strengths.

Denise Campbell thanks her grandmother, **Cecilia York**, for the world's best apple pie, teaching her how to cook, and that "you're never too old to learn."

To an inspired chef, **Cornelius P. McCarthy III**; he's a little messy but he's worth it! **Gail McCarthy**

In loving memory of **Bonnie Kennedy Beverly**, and in honor of my husband, **Whit**, and my mom, **Ginny Gordon**—you all inspire me to be the best I can be. **Julie Beverly**

Erin Downes honors her mother, **Joanne Downes**, for inspiring perseverance, commitment, and excellence.

To my mom, **Sheila Adams**, who gave me my endless imagination and ability to laugh at anything. With much love, **Maureen Adams Weaver**

Peggy Julicher honors her husband, **Hank**, for always being the wind beneath her wings.

Barbara Bashe honors the four generations of women that inspire her daily: **Isabelle Blakeslee, Kate Galen, Carol Galen, Lisa Galen,** and **Alexandra Bashe.**

To **Ruth** and **Jack Doyle**, my mother and father, my source of love and inspiration through the years. Heartfelt love and thanks, **Mary Liz Doyle Tadduni**

Peter, to a loving husband and father. You are our favorite cook! Thank you for keeping the Zelov family well fed. We love you. **Suzanne** and **Espy Zelov**

To my son, **Daniel**, the greatest joy of my life, and my husband, **Kenneth,** who feeds my spirit and nourishes my soul! All my love, **Maureen Huffman**

To my mother, **Mary Lou Walsh**: impromptu or planned, grand or small, your gatherings are always remembered by all. Love, your daughter, **Theresa Grabowski**

In loving memory of **Kimberly "Kimmy" Gregor**. Always the gracious hostess. Above all, a sweet, smiling friend with the kindest of all hearts. Love, **Janet Heaton**

In memory of my mother, **Betty Greenwell**, who taught me that there's always room for one more at the table, regardless of what's on the menu. With love, **Jane Greenwell Frantz**

In honor of my mother, **Mariann Bevan**, whose creativity always inspires me, my grandmother, **Laura M. Bevan**, who lovingly shared rich family traditions, and my babies, **Carter and Cameron**, who were with me from the inception of this project. With much love, **Cindy Bevan-Wilson**

To my mom, **Alice Comerford**, for her tireless compassion for life, commitment to family, and imparting the love of cooking! Bon Appétit, Mom, Love, **Colleen Comerford**

In memory of my grandmothers, **Mary Marshall Fritter** and **Louise Katherine Miller**, for filling me with "homemade love." **Leanne Miller Rush**

Thank you, **Janet Crovatto, Josephine Herrold, Carrie Crovatto**, and **Frieda Tettamanti**, for bestowing on me your knowledge of all things nourishing. With love, **Anne Bolton**

To my husband, **Arnie Schneider**, whose support has been so invaluable to The Saturday Club. With all my love, **Molly**

To my grandmother, **Sarah Sonntag**, the most gracious person I have ever known, and my mother, **Sally Gale,** for her constant love and dedication to our family. Love Always, **Lesley G. Blatchford**

Margaret Hondros honors her mother, **Helen Krill**, for all the gatherings around the dinner table and passing on the importance, and her love, of family.

To **The Saturday Club**: a gift to our community, a gift to women, and a gift to lasting friendship! Fondly, "The Main Line Classics"—**The Saturday Club Alumni:**

Allyson Hotz, Betty Ann Exler, Jean Kane, Karen Dalby, Doren Connors, Chappy Graf, Nancy Lawrence, Stacy Clark, Valerie Vitale, Nancy Hirschfeld, Sandy Lindberg, Anne Barker, Marita Needles, Denise Desatnick, Stacy Rohrbeck, Mary Liz Tadduni, Susan Connors, Jan McAllister, Corinne Ackerman, Gail Dewey, Babs Bickhart, Pat Leidy, Barbara Weber, Nancy Philips, Carrie Lawlor, Mary Ann Whalen, Karen Forcine, Shelley Heaberg, Maureen Katona, Jill Bonn, Barb Zonino, Julie Ferguson, Amy Hartsock, Julie Kincade, Cindy Williams, Kim Hildebrand, Stevie Lucas, Mary Ravenfeld, Kathy Shaw, Anne Taylor, Martha Thomson, Stacy Worback

DID YOU KNOW. . .

Since its founding in 1985, nonprofit Main Line Health has been fulfilling the mission of providing community-based health care to residents of the Main Line and beyond. As a charitable organization, the donations, revenues, and other forms of income received are reinvested in a continual effort to improve facilities and patient care.

More than 1,300 physicians and surgeons work side by side with other health care providers to deliver the highest possible quality of care. These dedicated professionals believe that each patient is unique, whether his or her need is a routine physical, complicated surgery, or sophisticated testing and diagnosis.

Over the course of a year, the Main Line Health hospitals:
- Admit almost 50,000 inpatients
- Deliver more than 5,500 babies
- Perform more than 28,000 surgeries
- Treat over 95,000 emergencies
- Provide more than 300,000 episodes of outpatient care.

Located in Philadelphia's western suburbs, Main Line Health offers easy access to three distinguished community-based acute care hospitals—Bryn Mawr, Lankenau, and Paoli—and a renowned specialty rehabilitation hospital, Bryn Mawr Rehab.

Other members of the Main Line Health family include centers in Exton, Lawrence Park (Broomall), Upper Providence and Shannondell at Valley Forge, as well as The Home Care Network, and other related subsidiaries.

Together, these facilities form a comprehensive network of inpatient, outpatient, home, and long-term care programs to meet virtually any medical need of its neighbors in the Main Line community.

To find a doctor or to learn more about Main Line Health, please call 1-866-CALL-MLH, or visit our website at www.mainlinehealth.org.

Main Line Health

Bryn Mawr Hospital
Lankenau Hospital
Paoli Hospital
Bryn Mawr Rehab Hospital

The Main Line Health Heart Center, a partnership of physicians at Lankenau, Bryn Mawr, and Paoli Hospitals, is nationally recognized for innovative and leading-edge cardiovascular research and medical education. Dedicated to reducing the impact of heart disease and improving the quality of life for those affected by it, the professionals at the Center provide a full continuum of care from prevention to heart transplantation.

Since 1979, Heart Center teams have performed more than 24,000 open-heart surgeries, making the facility one of the most trusted, experienced, and comprehensive centers in the Delaware Valley. The Center's mission is to provide the highest quality diagnosis, treatment, and rehabilitation in a patient-centered environment.

Community awareness is a critical component in the fight against cardiovascular disease. As part of this education effort, the Center is engaged in helping people identify and lower their risk of heart disease through Smart Heart, a community outreach program designed to promote heart-healthy lifestyles.

Choosing foods that taste good, and that are good for you, isn't always easy. That's why The Saturday Club enlisted the Main Line Health Heart Center to review this cookbook for heart-healthy menu options that are a part of any sound nutritional plan. Throughout these pages, Smart Heart recipes are identified by the Heart Center symbol ♡ .

We wish to thank Judy Matusky, RD, LDN, for leading this project. Judy, a nutrition educator for Main Line Health hospitals, provides personal nutrition counseling and lectures on issues such as weight management, women's health, and cardiovascular nutrition.

To find a doctor or to learn more about the Main Line Health Heart Center, call 1-866-CALL-MLH, or visit our website at www.mainlinehealth.org/heart.

Main Line Health

Heart Center

Lankenau Hospital
Bryn Mawr Hospital
Paoli Hospital

TABLE OF CONTENTS

FOOD
48

RECIPE KEY

Restaurant Contributors   Smart Heart Healthy   Make Ahead

The **Main Line**　　　Chamber of Commerce

Office of the President
Robert A. Pucci

January 2005

The *Main Line Entertains* cookbook is filled with elegant recipes and menus depicting various outings and entertaining venues throughout the Main Line area. We are very proud of the history and traditions that make the Main Line renowned around the world. But the Main Line of the twenty-first century enjoys the distinction of being one of the best places on earth in which to live, work, play, and learn.

Inside these pages, you will see images of horse races, rural farms, historic Main Line estates, tennis, historic landmarks, and farmers markets. You will enjoy learning about the lifestyles of many Main Liners and how they entertain.

Main Line Entertains will help preserve some of the area's culinary and entertaining traditions for both current and future generations—both within and outside of the Main Line itself.

The Main Line Chamber of Commerce commends The Saturday Club on its publication of *Main Line Entertains* and on its philanthropy in the region. As President and CEO of The Main Line Chamber of Commerce, I am excited about what this cookbook has to offer and proudly endorse *Main Line Entertains* as the "official cookbook of the twenty-first-century Main Line."

As you browse this cookbook and sample some of the wonderful recipes from the Main Line, you will, no doubt, understand why lifelong Main Liners like me like to say, "The best things in life…are here."

Sincerely,

Robert A. Pucci

175 Strafford Avenue, Suite 130, Wayne, PA 19087 / Phone: 610-687-6232 Fax: 610-687-8085

FOREWORD

The seeds of my culinary career were planted early, but took years to bear fruit. I remember well getting up early on Sunday mornings and being let loose in the kitchen to make breakfast before church. No pig at the proverbial trough was any happier than I. Being given the task of preparing a meal for six people might have been daunting for some twelve-year-olds, but for me, it was pure excitement. I would think all week about what I would make, read recipes, and finally on Sunday morning, I was Chef! Thirty-six years later, that excitement hasn't faded.

As I look back, I ask myself what made those experiences unforgettable. Was it putting together different ingredients that react with one another to create something that tastes good? Or was it the pleasure of watching someone eat and enjoy what I had made? For me then, as now, it was a bit of both.

I grew up in a large Catholic family during the era of *Leave It to Beaver*. In our home, planning a dinner party started weeks in advance with my mother's scrubbing of everything. I came to assume that the reason for having dinner parties was to have an incentive to clean the house! On the last day of the countdown, the bathroom was sterilized, and we were told to keep out. Monogrammed or embroidered hand towels that no one ever used were hung on the towel racks. Everyone, including the guests, understood that those towels were never to be touched. My wife carries on this tradition and it makes me wonder just what she thinks people are drying their hands on!

After attending a dinner at someone else's place, guests like to critique the party on their way home. The event's success is judged on how much the hosts have fussed, and the food, flowers, and music are all important parts of the formula. Entertaining is definitely a competitive art, and good hosts know that it's all in the details. But sometimes I wonder if cleaning the house after the party wouldn't make more sense so that one's energy could be put into the food!

Ever since my wife, Sue, and I opened Gilmore's in West Chester three years ago, we've never thought of it only as a restaurant, but a town home owned by a couple that likes to entertain a lot. We have felt as if we've been hosting one continuous dinner party.

A successful party elevates the spirit, enriches life, and enhances guests' self-esteem. We should entertain more often. How else are we going to get the house clean?

Peter Gilmore

THE SATURDAY CLUB

Established 1886

INTRODUCTION

Welcome to *Main Line Entertains*, a celebration of Main Line tradition and style. The Main Line was established in the late 1800s as a retreat from the city for wealthy Philadelphians. With the grand country homes came entertaining on a lavish scale. Times have changed, but the Main Line is still known for its legacy of gracious hospitality. The Saturday Club has contributed to that legacy with the publication of our wonderful cookbooks: *Main Line Classics* in 1982 and *Main Line Classics II: Cooking Up a Little History* in 1996. We are now thrilled to bring you this, our third cookbook.

Established in 1886 as a cultural and educational center by the wives of Wayne's businessmen, the Club has evolved into a nonprofit, philanthropic organization of 150 women who donate their time and energy to serve the greater Philadelphia area with both hands-on service and financial contributions to deserving nonprofit organizations. Our headquarters has served an integral role in the community since the late 1800s and is on the National Register of Historic Places. A significant portion of the funds we are able to distribute is generated through the sale of our cookbooks, so you are not only availing yourself of wonderful recipes, rich photography, and a wealth of entertaining knowledge, you are helping others in need.

We are so pleased to be able to share the history, the beauty, and the flavor of the Main Line with you. Enjoy!

Christine Kozeracki

Christine Kozeracki
President
The Saturday Club

ENTERTAINING MENUS

SPRING

Round-Robin Tennis Luncheon for Four

Devon Carriage Marathon Picnic for Twelve

Wedding Rehearsal Dinner for Thirty at Ardrossan

SUMMER

Seashore, Seashell, Seafood Avalon for Twelve

Summer Cocktails at Chanticleer for Twenty

Fourth of July Family Picnic for Eight

FALL

Brooke Farm Fall Festival

Radnor Hunt Three-Day Event Blue Ribbon Tailgate for Ten

Thanksgiving Dinner for Twelve

WINTER

Winter Brunch in the Kitchen for Eight

Elegant Dinner Party for Eight

Holiday Open House for Forty

ROUND-ROBIN TENNIS LUNCHEON FOR FOUR

Tennis is a very popular sport on the Main Line. Sunny spring mornings are perfect for The Round-Robin, a tournament where each contestant is matched in turn against every other contestant. Follow the fun with this light and refreshing spring luncheon menu.

SPRING FLINGS *(page 95)*

ICED TEA WITH STRAWBERRIES
& FRESH MINT

PAPAYA, CANTALOUPE &
HONEYDEW SKEWERS WITH
FRESH MINT & PROSCIUTTO *(page 66)*

TOMATO NAPOLEON WITH
FRESH TOMATO DRESSING ON A
BED OF SPRING GREENS *(page 114)*

CHICKEN MEDITERRANEAN SERVED OVER
BROILED POLENTA *(pages 159 and 137)*

STRAWBERRY HAZELNUT TORTA *(page 191)*

To make your very own tennis ball table, secure by placing glass votives upside down where place mats will be, fill in with tennis balls, and place a glass round on the tabletop. Substitute apples for a fall table, or baseballs for a Father's Day table, as other ways to create an eye-catching table.

DEVON CARRIAGE MARATHON
PICNIC FOR TWELVE

*The Devon Horse Show and Country Fair began in
1896 as a one-day show, the purpose of which
was to encourage local farmers to breed good horses,
especially carriage horses. After fifty years,
this philosophy produced the Devon Carriage Marathon,
which began in 1946 and is now known
as the Devon Pleasure Drive. The Carriage Marathon
is regarded internationally as a premier carriage event.
As it continues to evolve, participation is coveted
and limited to one hundred turnouts, generally considered
the very best in the carriage world.*

PIMM'S CUP *(page 94)*

PROSCIUTTO, GOAT CHEESE &
FRESH FIG ROLL-UPS *(page 67)*
SPICY GORGONZOLA SPREAD WITH
ROASTED RED PEPPERS *(page 80)*

MINTED CHICKEN & MELON SALAD *(page 104)*
SUMMER RICE SALAD *(page 118)*
SUMMER FRUIT WITH WINE & MINT *(page 186)*

LEMON STICKS *(page 189)*
JENNIFER'S JUMBLES *(page 199)*

*The Main Line Express Carriage is pulled by Rosemont,
Haverford, Strafford, and Radnor. Each horse is named
after a train station along the Main Line.*

SPRING

Wedding Rehearsal Dinner for Thirty at Ardrossan

Midori Champagne Cocktails *(page 93)*
Sand Castle Pinot Noir & Chardonnay Classic Wines

Lobster Quesadillas with Spicy Mango Salsa *(page 57)*
Red Pepper Gougères *(page 70)*
Wasabi Mussels *(page 63)*
Pear with Smoked Trout *(page 60)*
Sun-Dried Tomato & Brie Toasts *(page 73)*

Honeydew & White Wine Soup *(page 100)*

Citrus Asparagus Salad *(page 112)*

Pomegranate-Glazed Cornish Game Hens *(page 162)*
Balsamic-Glazed Baby Carrots *(page 122)*
Persian Rice *(page 138)*

Balsamic Strawberries over Sweet Mascarpone Cheese *(page 186)*
(Serve in a Champagne glass for an elegant presentation.)

At Ardrossan, lavish dinner parties as elegant as the one pictured here still take place today, and were customary when Hope Montgomery Scott was entertaining on the Main Line. Helen Hope Montgomery Scott was the oldest of four children of Colonel Robert L. Montgomery, head of a long-standing Philadelphia family. Born into a family of social prominence, Hope was in the forefront of wealthy Philadelphia society.

As the Main Line's most famous socialite, Hope was the model for the lead character in Philip Barry's 1939 play, The Philadelphia Story. Barry was a family friend and frequent visitor at Ardrossan. Later adapted for the silver screen, the award-winning movie of the same name starred Katherine Hepburn and broke box office records.

This photograph is sponsored by Wachovia Wealth Management.

SUMMER

SEASHORE, SEASHELL, SEAFOOD
AVALON FOR TWELVE

*The long, languid days of summer and dining alfresco
enhance even the best food. Tempt your guests with this
combination of icy libations, cool first-course selections, and
succulent offerings from the sea. Finish the feast with a
smooth dessert, brimming with the goodness of fruit in season.*

KEY LIME MARTINIS *(page 93)*

SAND CASTLE PINOT NOIR &
CHARDONNAY PRIVATE RESERVE WINES

MINIATURE CRAB CAKES WITH
TOMATO-GINGER COMPOTE *(page 56)*

RAW SEAFOOD BAR *(page 65)*

MANGO GAZPACHO SOUP GARNISHED
WITH GRILLED SHRIMP *(page 100)*

GLAZED TERIYAKI SALMON ON CRISPY POTATO
& SCALLION PANCAKES WITH RED & WHITE
PICKLED ONIONS *(pages 167, 129, and 141)*

ROASTED ASPARAGUS WITH LEMON
SAGE BUTTER *(page 119)*

GOLDEN COUSCOUS *(page 136)*

FROZEN LEMON TRIFLE WITH
FRESH SEASONAL BERRIES *(page 192)*

*About one hundred miles from the Main Line is a little slice
of heaven called the Jersey Shore, where family-oriented beach
communities line the southern coast of The Garden State.
From Cape May to Avalon to Long Beach Island, the coast
is peppered with favorite spots for Main Liners who like
to summer "down the shore." Another local linguistic
custom is shortening the term "Jersey Shore" to "The Shore"
and referring to the state of New Jersey simply as "Jersey."*

SUMMER

SUMMER COCKTAILS AT CHANTICLEER FOR TWENTY

A themed cocktail party is always fun. This menu features many Asian appetizers that can be easily eaten while standing at a cocktail party. Try serving the Spicy Thai Noodle Salad in small individual bowls or nested in individual Asian soup spoons.

SAND CASTLE CHARDONNAY CLASSIC AND JOHANNISBERG RIESLING WINES
GINGER MARTINIS *(page 92)*

SESAME CHICKEN SKEWERS *(page 63)*
PORK DUMPLINGS WITH CHEF VAL'S GINGER SOY DIPPING SAUCE *(page 62)*
SEARED SPICE-ENCRUSTED TUNA WITH PINEAPPLE PEPPERCORN SALSA
ON A CHIVE RICE PATTY *(page 58)*
ASIAN BARBECUED RACK OF LAMB *(page 152)*
SPICY THAI NOODLE SALAD *(page 117)*
SUMMER SPRING ROLLS *(page 60)*

BITTERSWEET CHOCOLATE FONDUE WITH POMEGRANATE SYRUP
IN BENTO BOXES FILLED WITH FORTUNE COOKIES,
FRESH ASIAN PEARS & SEASONAL FRUIT *(page 182)*
(Served with chopsticks…of course.)

Nestled in the suburbs of Philadelphia lies a thirty-five acre estate named "Chanticleer," once inhabited by the Rosengarten family. When their son died in 1990, the acreage became part of the Chanticleer Charitable Trust and Foundation. What was once a gentleman's estate is now referred to as a "pleasure garden," replete with woodland walks, a rolling hill, a "ruin" garden with a mystical water table, splendid vistas, and an aquatic garden that is without peer in the Greater Philadelphia area.

Appreciated by ladies who lunch and families alike, the gardens at Chanticleer are the perfect setting for a leisurely stroll that takes one back to a more refined, genteel time. During the summer months, Main Line families and friends come to Chanticleer to stroll the garden on Friday nights, taking in the horticultural gem that lies right in their backyard.

SUMMER

FOURTH OF JULY FAMILY PICNIC FOR EIGHT

All the appetizers and desserts in this menu can be made ahead of time...freeing you up to enjoy your family and friends. In fact, the Summertime Vegetable Caponata tastes best when it marinates for two to three days before serving.

ADULT WATERMELON LEMONADE *(page 96)*
ASSORTED CHERRY & RASPBERRY SODAS
LOCAL BEER & SAND CASTLE WINE

TEQUILA FIRE SHRIMP ON CURVED SKEWERS *(page 64)*
SUMMERTIME VEGETABLE CAPONATA IN A BOWL
WITH SLICED BAGUETTE *(page 73)*

BRAZILIAN POTATO SALAD *(page 113)*
CHILIED FLANK STEAK *(page 147)*
MEXICAN GRILLED CORN *(page 123)*
POINT-TO-POINT SALAD WITH SPICY CASHEWS *(page 108)*

RITA'S WATER ICE IN LEMON SHELLS *(page 198)*
SINFUL COCOA BROWNIES *(page 197)*

VALLEY FORGE NATIONAL HISTORICAL PARK

General George Washington chose the wheat fields of Valley Forge as the winter encampment of the Continental Army in December 1777. "Firecakes," a flour-and-water mixture cooked over a campfire, helped to sustain the army through the harsh Pennsylvania winter. The time spent at Valley Forge toughened the soldiers, as the camp lacked adequate shelter, and food and clothing were in short supply. When spring came around, the Continental Army had been conditioned by the elements and began to win battle after battle, and eventually the war.

Today, people come here to remember this part of our patriotic past. They picnic in the park while reading the many monuments' tributes to the soldiers and give thanks to those who sacrificed so much for our freedom.

FALL

BROOKE FARM
FALL FESTIVAL

*Halloween neighborhood block parties are popular
on the Main Line, with both adults and kids dressing up.
The clove-studded apples and oranges in this Fall Cider
Punch provide a decorative touch all their own, so choose a clear
glass punch bowl to show off these beautiful harvest hues!
This menu is sure to be a big hit at your next fall party.*

LOCAL BEER & FALL CIDER PUNCH *(page 96)*

PUMPKIN PARMESAN TOASTS WITH
HERB PESTO *(page 72)*
CANNELLINI BEAN DIP, SERVED IN
SMALL PUMPKIN SHELLS *(page 79)*
SPICY CASHEWS *(page 81)*

CURRIED PUMPKIN &
SWEET POTATO SOUP *(page 103)*

PORK MEDALLIONS WITH
CIDER SAUCE *(page 155)*
APPLE SLAW *(page 112)*
ROASTED PEAR & BLUE CHEESE SALAD *(page 110)*
RUSTIC BREAD

CARROT CAKE SANDWICH COOKIES *(page 200)*
GINGER CRACK COOKIES *(page 201)*

*Samuel Brooke built a house and barn in 1771,
located at the corner of Brooke and Church Roads
in St. David's. The barn appears today much
as it did in the 1880s, and is the setting
of our elegant Halloween party seen here.*

FALL

RADNOR HUNT THREE-DAY EVENT BLUE RIBBON
TAILGATE FOR TEN

*Every October, Olympians and their world-class horses come to bucolic Willistown Township
in Malvern, Pennsylvania, to compete in the Radnor Hunt International Three-Day Event.
Benefiting the Special Olympics of Chester County, the first day of this rigorous competition sees
spectators, sponsors, and often their dogs gathering on the beautiful hillsides of Radnor Hunt's country
property to enjoy the sport. Equestrian excellence is the star attraction, but there is also a country fair with
food, interesting shops, and pony rides. At noon on the final day, the Pet Parade attracts various species
of contestants to compete in classes such as best owner and pet look-alike, most exotic, and cutest puppy.
On Sunday afternoon, those who participate in the annual themed tailgate competition invite
a group of friends to join them on the rail to party. Their bonus: an excellent view of the
stadium-jumping event, which determines the overall winner of the competition.*

FALL

THANKSGIVING DINNER FOR TWELVE

After your family and guests have had a chance to digest their Thanksgiving meal, bring out a tray with hollowed-out pumpkins and gourds of various sizes lined with plastic wrap and filled with whipped cream, sugar cubes, cinnamon sticks, miniature marshmallows, chocolate curls, or chocolate-dipped spoons to serve with coffee and hot chocolate.

SAND CASTLE WINES & CRANBERRY KIR ROYALE *(page 91)*

SAVORY FRESH HERB CHEESECAKE *(page 77)*

MUSHROOMS IN PHYLLO CUPS *(page 55)*

ARUGULA & LEAFY GREENS WITH PARMESAN
BOW TIES & BALSAMIC APPLE VINAIGRETTE *(page 107)*

ROASTED HERB TURKEY WITH CARAMELIZED
ONION & BALSAMIC GRAVY *(page 163)*

PENNSYLVANIA FARMHOUSE STUFFING *(page 140)*

CRANBERRY-ORANGE RELISH *(page 141)*

PEAS WITH PANCETTA *(page 126)*

SWEET POTATO & APPLE GRATIN *(page 131)*

BASIC GARLIC MASHED POTATOES *(page 130)*

FRENCH GREEN BEANS WITH PEARS
& PARMESAN *(page 120)*

PUMPKIN PIE WITH MAPLE-PECAN STREUSEL *(page 205)*

HONEY APPLE TORTE *(page 190)*

Wine is a frequent companion to good food, and the right wine can enhance the flavors of your meal. A crisp riesling provides balance for spicy foods and Oriental cuisines, as well as fruits such as melon, cantaloupe, pineapple, and tangerines. The silky chardonnay is a versatile choice for many foods and is traditionally served with grilled chicken and pork, or seafood offerings such as tuna or swordfish. A fruity pinot noir is wonderful when paired with game such as venison or duck, and complements an oily fish like salmon, too. The smooth, more complex cabernet sauvignon can easily stand up to dishes such as red meat, lamb, or hearty pastas.

35

WINTER

WINTER BRUNCH IN THE KITCHEN
FOR EIGHT

Although this menu is perfect for conquering the winter doldrums, it works just as well to celebrate the first warm rays of spring. Served in the late morning (hence its name), brunch promotes a relaxed atmosphere and is enjoyed by all. When the weekend rolls around, you can enjoy this leisurely meal at your favorite diner or café, or plan your own using make-ahead dishes like the ones here! Whether sweet treats make you swoon or there is a hankering for omelets, this brunch menu will satisfy even the pickiest palate. After such a delightful meal, the only hard part will be finding someone to do the dishes.

HONEY BRUNCH MIMOSAS *(page 94)*
COFFEE & TEA
FRESH SQUEEZED JUICES

MAPLE PECAN BACON *(page 84)*
FIESTA FRITTATA *(page 86)*
CHICKEN SALAD WITH ROASTED ASPARAGUS
& TOASTED ALMONDS *(page 104)*
POPOVER PANCAKE *(page 89)*

MIXED BERRIES WITH LEMON CREAM *(page 87)*
WALNUT PEAR SOUR CREAM CAKE *(page 88)*

Flowers are essential to entertaining and can truly make your gathering special. For our winter brunch, we used antique china cups and teapots and tightly filled them with Helleborus 'Christmas Glory', a deep ruby-colored flower. Another elegant winter look can be achieved by filling glass vases with cranberries and then adding white roses or lilies.

The mountain laurel (Kalmia latifolia) is the official state flower of Connecticut, Pennsylvania, and The Saturday Club. This beautiful woodland shrub is native to America and is appreciated for its fragrant, massive clusters of white and pink blossoms.

W I N T E R

Elegant Dinner Party for Eight

*Turn up the heat on a cold February night with this luscious array of foods
sure to stoke the fires of true love. For a welcome change from the usual crowded restaurant,
invite a few close friends to your home for an intimate Valentine's Day dinner.
Decorate your table with colors and symbols of this holiday for sweethearts,
and create warm memories for everyone in attendance.*

Recipe for Romance:
*Arrange votives throughout the house for a soft glow. Load your CD player with pop standards
by greats like Nat King Cole and Frank Sinatra. Meet each guest at the door with a glass of Champagne
(a teaspoon or two of pomegranate juice in each flute turns the bubbly into a rosy cocktail).
Voilà! Instant atmosphere!*

CHAMPAGNE
SAND CASTLE CABERNET SAUVIGNON

SPINACH SALAD WITH FRIED BLUE CHEESE *(page 109)*
ROASTED RACK OF LAMB WITH ROSEMARY-GARLIC SAUCE *(page 151)*
BAKED HERB-STUFFED TOMATOES *(page 132)*
ORZO WITH CARAMELIZED ONIONS *(page 136)*

PEAR SORBET *(page 188)*
WARM CHOCOLATE CAKES GARNISHED WITH
FRESH RASPBERRIES & A DOLLOP OF WHIPPED CREAM *(page 194)*

> *Few things are more romantic than sharing this warm
> cake, oozing with dark chocolate and topped with Kahlúa
> whipped cream. The perfect dessert for chocoholics.*

WINTER

HOLIDAY OPEN HOUSE FOR FORTY

During the holiday season, an open house is a wonderful way to entertain on a large scale.
This menu is sure to please, and can be set on several buffet tables for a casual atmosphere.
For a dressier affair, have your appetizers butlered.

When entertaining a varied group of revelers, you'll be set with this adaptable menu, filled with simply elegant
and easy-to-prepare dishes. Take advantage of the many items that can be made ahead, and adjust
your quantities to accommodate larger or smaller crowds.

The finishing touches are holiday music, greenery, and a snowflake or two for the perfect holiday party!

SAND CASTLE CHARDONNAY PRIVATE RESERVE & CABERNET SAUVIGNON WINES
BRANDYWINE PUNCH *(page 97)* ▪ FULLY STOCKED BAR

CANDY BACON DATES *(page 66)*
GOAT CHEESE TORTA WITH HOMEMADE PITA CHIPS *(page 79)*
WARM EXOTIC MUSHROOM SPREAD WITH CROSTINI *(page 71)*
FINGERLING POTATOES WITH CAVIAR *(page 69)*
ROASTED PEPPER & ARTICHOKE TAPENADE *(page 74)*
PROSCIUTTO-WRAPPED ASPARAGUS SPEARS *(page 67)*
APRICOT PECAN BRIE TARTLETS, PANCETTA, LEEK &
GOAT CHEESE TARTLETS, & RASPBERRY & BRIE TARTLETS *(pages 54 and 55)*
BELGIUM ENDIVE SPEARS WITH DUCK & APRICOT *(page 61)*

RASPBERRY-MARINATED BEEF TENDERLOIN *(page 144)*
BAY LEAF RED-SKINNED ROASTED POTATOES *(page 128)*
ROASTED VEGETABLE TIMBALES *(page 135)*
APPLE CHERRY WALNUT SALAD WITH CREAMY MAPLE DRESSING *(page 111)*

TIRAMISU EGGNOG TRIFLE *(page 192)* ▪ ASSORTMENT OF CHOCOLATE TRUFFLES
BANANA BUNDLES WITH CHOCOLATE GANACHE *(page 187)*

The holiday "Open House" is the classic way to kick off the high season of home entertaining.
It's a wonderful opportunity to be surrounded by friends, both old and new, as well as neighbors
and co-workers. Opening your home is a most gracious way to spread the holiday spirit.

E N T E R

In *Main Line Entertains*, we provide you with some wonderful entertaining ideas and twelve menus to complement your events.

Entertaining is about being with friends and having a good time, not perfect silver and china! Use what you have to set the table. Make it festive with flowers and candles, enjoy the company of good friends and family, and most of all, have fun!

Gracious hosts are relaxed and greet their guests at the door. Selecting menu items that are ready before guests arrive allows you to spend time with them instead of being confined in the kitchen. Recipes marked by a train track ( ) are especially suited to advance preparation so that last minute meal details are kept to a minimum. Consider hiring one or two people to serve so you can concentrate on your most important duty: being a host! Hosting duties include introducing your guests to others and making everyone feel welcome. A great introduction includes a little information about each person so guests have a place to begin their own conversation.

T A I N !

INVITATION ETIQUETTE

Invitations take many forms today. For a casual event, a phone call may be enough to serve as an invitation. Sending a handmade or printed invitation in the mail is still the preferred way to invite guests. We all like seeing those pretty envelopes arrive; it makes us feel special!

When writing an invitation, be sure to include the date, time, place, name of the person hosting the event, type of dress (casual, cocktail attire, black tie, etc.), and RSVP options. Invitations should be received at least two weeks prior to the event, and the RSVP date should be clearly stated. RSVP is an acronym for the French *répondez s'il vous plaît*, meaning "respond if you please."

So now you are ready to entertain...

SELECT A PARTY THEME

To make the party truly your own, get creative and try one of these party themes:

▪ AROUND THE WORLD PARTY

Go international by making each room in your home suggest a different country. Have the décor, food, and drink fit that country. For an Indian theme, place large pillows on the floor. Create a fiesta with sombreros and maracas. Make a stop in Paris for dessert and espresso. Hand out little charms as mementos to your guests for visiting each country. Make this a night to remember.

PROGRESSIVE DINNER

Progressive Dinner is a favorite party theme for Saturday Club members and Main Line neighbor communities. Gather your neighborhood together, or any other large group, for an evening of convivial cooking, dining, and entertaining on the move. Everyone meets in one home for cocktails and appetizers. The group then breaks down into smaller individual dinner parties at other homes. After dinner, the groups reconvene en masse in another home for coffee and dessert. All who attend share the cooking, and the same menu is served at each dinner, with the cooking assignments distributed before the event. Dinner seating assignments can be prearranged, or for a fun twist, have the dinner hosts pull their guests' names from a hat during cocktails! This is a great way to get to know a group better.

ENTER

■ **COOKIE EXCHANGE**

Cut down on your baking time by hosting a festive cookie exchange party. Invite five friends over and have each bring six dozen cookies. Everyone keeps a dozen of each variety, and best of all, you can exchange recipes. Be sure to try our special Ginger Crack Cookies on page 201. This is a great party to host at the holidays so you have a variety of sweet treats for guests when they drop by.

■ **DISCO CLUB**

Invite everyone to your "club," and make sure there are bouncers and great music. Serve food from the 1970s, such as our Bittersweet Chocolate Fondue with Pomegranate Syrup on page 182 and our Updated "Pigs in a Blanket" on page 70.

■ **HAWAIIAN LUAU**

Host a pig roast with great tropical drinks and plenty of torches, dancers in grass skirts and leis, and Lobster Quesadillas with Spicy Mango Salsa on page 57. Serve the salsa in a pineapple sliced lengthwise and hollowed out.

■ **MIDSUMMER'S EVE PARTY**

Go Shakespearean and provide floral head wreaths (chaplets) for your guests. Serve a whole pig cooked on a spit over an open fire, along with our Marinated Butterflied Leg of Lamb on page 152. The Frozen Lemon Trifle on page 192 for dessert will top off a special night.

■ **MONTE CARLO NIGHT**

Turn your home into a casino, complete with gaming tables throughout the house. If you choose to go the James Bond route, you can ask the men to wear black tie and have a martini bar with the different martinis named for Bond movies. An ice sculpture with an Ace and King design makes a great martini "luge." Cigars and brandy are perfect for the patio or porch. The music, food, and décor should have a Mediterranean theme as well. Our Fingerling Potatoes with Caviar appetizer on page 69 will be a sure hit with your James Bond crowd.

Now all you need to do is decide if you want to host a buffet or sit-down affair…

BUFFETS

Buffets are a convenient way to serve food to a large group. Make sure the food is served in bite-size pieces if guests will not be seated at a dining table, so they don't have to worry about balancing a plate, a knife, and a fork! To make your buffet table inviting, use low votive candles and flowers strewn around the table. Place your serving containers at various heights to create visual interest. Always provide a table or an area where dirty dishes are to be collected. And remember: never put any dirty dishes, glasses, or napkins back on the buffet table!

Buffet means "sideboard" in French; therefore, the food is placed on a side table for self-service. According to legend, Ben Franklin invented this serving method out of necessity when he was visiting in France and had to entertain members of the French Court but had no suitable furniture. He took a board, placed it on a table up against a wall, and covered it, creating a "buffet."

Dinner plates should be in stacks of no more than eight at the end of the table, and guests should move along the buffet from left to right. The main course should be hot and bite-size, able to be eaten with only a fork, and placed next to the dinner plates. Guests serve themselves and move down the line to the other dishes. The silverware and napkins should be at the end of the buffet table.

For an informal buffet dinner, guests would then move to chairs, couches, and even stairs to find a place to sit and eat. To formalize your buffet, set a table with complete place settings of silverware, glasses, and napkins. Your guests may serve themselves at the buffet and then take their seats at the table.

Additional side tables may be used for coffee, tea, other beverages, and desserts. For the convenience of your guests, you might set up a separate table for dirty dishes and the like.

NAPKIN ETIQUETTE

Yes, there is such a thing as napkin etiquette, and it is the same for paper or cloth napkins.

When seated at a table, and after your host/hostess picks up his/her napkin, pick up your napkin and immediately put it in your lap. Do not flap it in the air to open it, but do so discreetly under the table so that the fold of the napkin faces your waist. This allows you to lift a corner of the napkin to blot your mouth throughout the meal.

When you need to leave the table for only a few moments, your napkin is placed on your dining chair. At the end of the meal, the hostess will pick up her napkin at the center and place it loosely to the left of her plate.

Formal Sit-Down Affairs

SOME GENERAL RULES INCLUDE:

- Forks go on the left (except the seafood cocktail fork, which goes on the right).
- Knives go on the right with the blade facing the plate.
- Soup spoons go to the right of the knife. A round soup spoon is for clear or creamed soup, and an oval soup spoon is for thicker, chunky soups.
- Teaspoons should be served with the coffee or tea.
- A butter spreader is a little knife that goes on your bread plate, always on your left. (Tip to remember: "food" has four letters, "left" has four letters, and food such as salad or bread is served on the left.)
- Drinks are always on your right and are served from the right. (Tip to remember: "drink" has five letters, "right" has five letters!) Water glasses are the largest and are placed at the tip of the knife. Wine glasses are placed to the right of the water glass in the order in which they will be served.
- Always work from the outside in toward the plate. For example, if you have a salad fork and a dinner fork at your place setting, and the salad is served first, the salad fork will be to the left of the dinner fork.
- A dessert spoon and/or dessert fork may be placed above the plate at the top of the place setting. If the dessert spoon and fork arrive on the dessert plate, or are placed above the dinner plate, you should move the fork to your left and place the spoon on your right for the dessert course.
- Don't put the napkin under the forks because you do not want guests to have to pick up the silverware to reach their forks.
- Etiquette rule: Once you pick up a piece of silverware, it never again goes back on the table, but must be placed on a plate.

UNIQUE TABLE FAVORS ARE A WAY TO MAKE YOUR EVENT TRULY MEMORABLE

Table favors are small gifts for your guests to take home. Some fun ideas include:

- A CD of music from your party, or favorite songs of the guest of honor
- A recipe box with a copy of the menu and recipes served at your party
- A small garden pot with packages of seeds or potted herbs
- A small picture frame
- A spoon dipped in chocolate
- Chocolate truffles
- Cinnamon sticks tied together with a pretty bow
- Miniature bottles of Champagne

GUEST ETIQUETTE

So, you are invited to a special party! How wonderful!

Remember to always RSVP in a timely fashion. No one likes to have to call the invited guests to see if they are indeed coming to the party! Dress up and dress appropriately, as this shows respect for your host and hostess. Arrive on time or within fifteen minutes of the announced time, and bring a small hostess gift. Some fun and sure-to-be-appreciated gifts include:

- A bottle of wine, which can be enjoyed at a later date
- A lovely coffee table book
- Aromatic candles
- Assorted candies
- A Silpat baking mat and shaped cookie cutters
- An assortment of gourmet coffees or teas
- A small plant
- A specialized book about drinks for the bar area
- Flowers (already arranged so the hostess does not have to search for a vase)
- Lovely guest towels for the powder room
- Personalized stationery
- An assortment of flavored vinegars and olive oils

THE SATURDAY CLUB'S CLUBHOUSE

Nestled within Philadelphia's Main Line, a unique community of elegant stone mansions, historic churches, and quaint railroad stations, is The Saturday Club clubhouse, a charming Tudor-style cottage that is available even today to rent for your Main Line entertaining parties and events!

Our clubhouse has a capacity for 150 guests, is the perfect setting for entertaining, and features cathedral ceilings and window seats, an ornamental fireplace, a grand piano on an elevated stage, a full kitchen, and a beautiful ballroom with hardwood floors. The clubhouse's amenities make it suitable for all types of functions: wedding receptions, rehearsal dinners, corporate meetings, seminars, fund-raisers, Bar/Bat Mitzvahs, Communions, family reunions, birthday parties, and dances. You have the choice of time, date, and caterer for your event!

As a 501(c)(3) nonprofit organization, the best part about renting the Saturday Club's clubhouse is that the proceeds go right back into the community. To look inside our beautiful clubhouse or for more information, please visit our website: www.saturdayclub.org, or call (610) 688-9746.

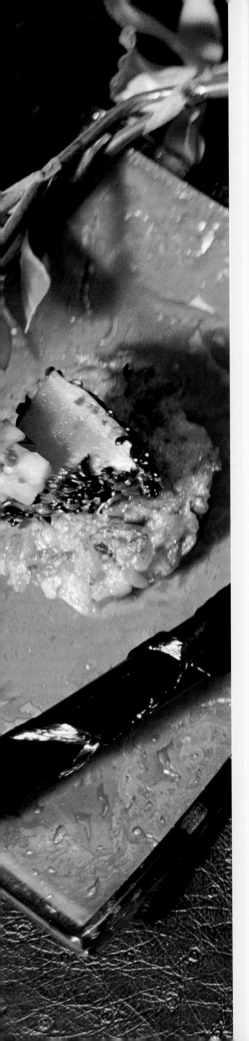

FOOD

APPETIZERS

BRUNCH &
BEVERAGES

SOUPS · SALADS
SIDE DISHES

MAIN DISHES

DESSERTS

49

ARDMORE FARMERS MARKET

*Built in celebration of Suburban Square's 75th Anniversary,
the Ardmore Farmers Market incorporates historic elements
with modern sophistication. The adjacent parking lot, indoor and outdoor
dining terraces, wide shopping aisles, and extended operating hours provide convenience
and ease, while the vaulted beam ceilings with clerestory windows and
blonde maple wood highlights frame the merchants' fresh offerings.
A mosaic of color and taste, the market's vendors offer an expansive selection
of fresh produce, seafood, and culinary masterpieces of the "ready to serve" fashion.
The Ardmore Farmers Market enables shoppers to savor meals
at home or dine "on the run" from nineteen stands.*

LANCASTER COUNTY FARMERS MARKET

The Lancaster County Farmers Market originated over sixty years ago as a collection of stands where the farmers of Lancaster County would sell their meat, produce, and handcrafts to the residents of Philadelphia and the Main Line. Vendors made their way to Rosemont two days a week, which left the other days free for harvesting fruits, trimming meats, and preparing the goods to be sold. The market grew and eventually moved to its current location on Lancaster Avenue in Strafford-Wayne, and demand is such that the market is now open three days each week—Wednesday, Friday, and Saturday.

The Lancaster County Farmers Market is a truly special place to many Main Line residents and has been a regular stop for families on Saturday mornings for generations. As you enter the building, you are greeted by the wonderful smells of freshly baked pastries, breads, pretzels, bacon, cinnamon French toast, roasting chickens, coffee, and "party dogs." Without a doubt, you will run into friends having breakfast and shopping at the dozens of family-owned businesses that offer a dizzying variety of foods, flowers, and gifts. A great cup of coffee and lots of happy people—not a bad way to start the day!

APPETIZERS

Apricot Pecan Brie Tartlets

1 (8-ounce) wheel Brie cheese, chilled
1 1/2 (17-ounce) packages frozen puff pastry sheets, thawed
1/4 cup apricot preserves
24 pecan halves

Preheat the oven to 425 degrees. Remove the rind from the cheese and cut into 24 cubes. Roll the pastry into a 10×15-inch rectangle on a lightly floured surface and cut into 24 squares. Fit the squares into miniature muffin cups, extending the corners over the rims. Bake for 10 to 12 minutes or until puffed and light brown.

Remove from the oven and gently press the handle of a wooden spoon into the center of each pastry to form a shell. Fill each shell with 1/2 teaspoon of the preserves. Top each with a cheese cube and a pecan half. Bake for 5 minutes or until the cheese melts. Serve immediately.

Note: You may use miniature phyllo pastry shells instead of the puff pastry.

Makes 2 dozen tartlets

Pancetta, Leek & Goat Cheese Tartlets

2 tablespoons butter
2 cups chopped leeks (white and pale
   green parts only, about 3 large)
1 teaspoon vegetable oil
4 ounces thinly sliced pancetta, chopped
24 miniature phyllo shells

2/3 cup half-and-half
2 egg yolks
1/4 teaspoon salt
1/8 teaspoon freshly ground pepper
2 ounces soft fresh goat cheese, crumbled

Preheat the oven to 350 degrees. Melt the butter in a large skillet over medium heat. Add the leeks and sauté for 10 minutes. Remove from the heat to cool. Heat the oil in a small skillet over medium-high heat. Add the pancetta and sauté for 6 minutes or until crisp. Remove the pancetta with a slotted spoon to drain on paper towels.

Place the phyllo shells on a baking sheet. Whisk the half-and-half, egg yolks, salt and pepper in a medium bowl until blended. Stir in the goat cheese, leeks and pancetta. Spoon into the phyllo shells. Bake for 30 minutes or until the filling is set and the edges are golden brown. Cool in the pans for 5 minutes. (You may make 1 day ahead and cover and chill on the baking sheet. Reheat, uncovered, in a preheated 350-degree oven for 12 minutes before serving.)

Note: Pancetta is bacon cured in salt and is available at Italian markets and specialty foods stores.

Makes 2 dozen tartlets

RASPBERRY & BRIE TARTLETS

I (8-ounce) wheel Brie cheese
24 miniature phyllo shells

2 tablespoons raspberry preserves
72 sliced almonds

Preheat the oven to 350 degrees. Remove the rind from the cheese and cut the cheese into 24 small pieces. Place the phyllo shells on a baking sheet and fill each with a scant $1/4$ teaspoon of the preserves. Top each with a small piece of cheese and 3 sliced almonds. Bake for 15 minutes or until the cheese melts.

Note: You may purchase fresh phyllo dough from your Greek grocer and prepare your own phyllo shells.

Makes 2 dozen tartlets

MUSHROOMS IN PHYLLO CUPS

PHYLLO CUPS
I (16-ounce) package phyllo dough, thawed
$1/4$ cup ($1/2$ stick) butter, melted

FILLING
5 tablespoons unsalted butter
$1/4$ cup minced onion
I pound mushrooms, finely chopped
$1/2$ tablespoon all-purpose flour
$1/2$ cup (or less) half-and-half
$1/2$ teaspoon salt
$1/8$ teaspoon cayenne pepper

$1/4$ teaspoon black pepper
$1 1/2$ teaspoons chopped fresh chives
2 tablespoons chopped fresh parsley
I teaspoon lemon juice
3 tablespoons freshly grated Parmesan
    cheese (optional)

For the phyllo cups, preheat the oven to 350 degrees. Brush I sheet of the pastry with melted butter, keeping the remaining pastry covered with a damp cloth. Cut the pastry with a sharp knife into 2-inch squares. Layer 4 buttered pastry squares at slightly different angles in each of 36 miniature muffin cups. Repeat until all of the pastry has been used. Bake for 6 to 8 minutes or until golden brown. Carefully remove from the cups and cool on a wire rack. Maintain the oven temperature.

For the filling, melt the butter in a skillet. Add the onion and sauté for 3 minutes. Add the mushrooms and sauté for 15 minutes or until the liquid evaporates. Remove from the heat and sprinkle with the flour. Mix well and add the half-and-half. Cook until the mixture is very thick, stirring constantly. Remove from the heat. Add the salt, cayenne pepper, black pepper, chives, parsley and lemon juice and mix well.

To assemble, place the phyllo cups on a baking sheet and fill with the mushroom mixture. Sprinkle with the Parmesan cheese and bake for 10 minutes. (You may make ahead and freeze in an airtight container before baking the second time. To serve, place on a baking sheet and bake for 20 minutes.)

Note: When working with phyllo dough, keep the dough moist by covering the sheets with a damp towel to prevent them from drying out.

Makes 3 dozen tartlets

Miniature Crab Cakes with Tomato-Ginger Compote

Tomato-Ginger Compote

1/4 cup minced shallot
2 tablespoons minced fresh ginger
I garlic clove, minced
3/4 teaspoon salt
1/4 teaspoon black pepper
1/8 teaspoon red pepper flakes

2 tablespoons butter
I tablespoon sugar
I 1/2 pounds canned plum tomatoes
I 1/2 tablespoons lime juice
2 tablespoons chopped fresh cilantro

Crab Cakes

I red bell pepper, minced
I tablespoon sesame oil
1/4 cup mayonnaise
I egg yolk
I 1/2 tablespoons Dijon mustard
2 tablespoons lemon juice

3/4 teaspoon dried tarragon
I tablespoon minced fresh ginger
I pound lump crab meat, shells removed
I cup unseasoned panko (Japanese
   bread crumbs)

For the compote, sauté the shallot, ginger, garlic, salt, black pepper and red pepper flakes in the butter in a skillet over medium heat for 5 minutes or until softened. Add the sugar and cook until dissolved, stirring constantly. Add the tomatoes and simmer for 15 to 20 minutes over low heat until thickened, stirring constantly. Stir in the lime juice and cilantro just before serving. (You may make the compote I day ahead.)

For the crab cakes, sauté the bell pepper in the sesame oil in a skillet over medium-high heat for 2 minutes or until soft and golden brown. Whisk the mayonnaise, egg yolk, mustard, lemon juice, tarragon and ginger in a large bowl. Fold in the panko. Stir in the sautéed bell pepper. Stir in the crab meat gently. (You may make the crab cakes I day ahead up to this point.) Preheat the oven to 350 degrees. Drop the crab meat mixture by rounded teaspoonfuls onto a baking sheet. Bake for 12 minutes or until golden brown and heated through.

To serve, top each crab cake with a dollop of the compote.

Makes 40 crab cakes

LOBSTER QUESADILLAS WITH SPICY MANGO SALSA

MANGO SALSA
4 very ripe mangoes, chopped
1/2 fresh pineapple, chopped
I red onion, chopped
1/2 red bell pepper, chopped
I bunch fresh cilantro, chopped
I teaspoon salt
1/2 teaspoon Tabasco sauce
Juice of I lime

QUESADILLAS
2/3 cup shredded Monterey Jack cheese
1/3 cup shredded jalapeño Monterey Jack cheese
2 steamed or boiled lobster tails, chopped
1/2 onion, chopped
3 tablespoons chopped scallions
2 teaspoons chopped red bell pepper
4 (9-inch) flour tortillas
1/4 cup vegetable oil

SERVING SUGGESTION

For an elegant serving presentation, slice a whole pineapple into halves lengthwise, including the green top. Remove the pulp from 1 pineapple half and chop to use in the salsa, reserving the shell. Reserve the remaining pineapple half for another use. Spoon the salsa into the reserved pineapple shell and place in the center of a serving platter. Cut the quesadillas into quarters and arrange around the pineapple. Garnish with cilantro.

For the salsa, combine the mangoes, pineapple, onion, bell pepper, cilantro, salt, Tabasco sauce and lime juice in a bowl and mix well.

For the quesadillas, mix the Monterey Jack cheese and jalapeño Monterey Jack cheese in a bowl. Layer 1/2 of the cheese, the lobster, onion, scallions, bell pepper and remaining 1/2 of cheese mixture evenly on each of 2 of the tortillas. Top each with the remaining tortillas. Heat the oil in a skillet until hot but not smoking. Add the quesadillas. Cook until brown on each side, turning once. Serve with the salsa.

Variation:
For Grilled Chicken Quesadillas, cut 2 grilled boneless skinless chicken breasts into bite-size pieces and use instead of the lobster.

Serves 4

Seared Spice-Encrusted Tuna with Pineapple Peppercorn Salsa on a Chive Rice Patty

Chive Rice Patties

2 cups water
Salt to taste
1 cup long grain white rice
2 eggs
1 cup chopped fresh chives

1/2 cup all-purpose flour
1 teaspoon baking powder
2 teaspoons sea salt
1/2 cup peanut oil

Tuna

1 1/2 cups pineapple juice
1/2 cup soy sauce
2 tablespoons brown sugar
1 teaspoon grated fresh garlic
1 teaspoon grated fresh ginger
4 (1 1/2×1 1/2×6-inch) logs of sushi
   grade tuna

2 tablespoons coarsely crushed pink
   peppercorns
2 tablespoons coarsely crushed anise seeds
2 tablespoons nigella seeds
1/4 cup black sesame seeds
1/4 cup white sesame seeds
2/3 cup peanut oil

Pineapple Peppercorn Salsa

1 cup finely chopped fresh pineapple
2 1/2 tablespoons very finely chopped red
   onion
1 tablespoon fresh mint, cut in a fine
   chiffonade

2 teaspoons grated fresh ginger
2 teaspoons minced fresh ginger
4 teaspoons whole pink peppercorns
1/4 teaspoon salt

For the chive rice patties, bring 2 cups salted water to a boil in a saucepan. Stir in the rice and reduce the heat. Simmer for 15 to 20 minutes or until the water is absorbed. Cool the rice in a large bowl. Mix the eggs and chives in a small bowl. Mix the flour, baking powder and 2 teaspoons sea salt together. Add the egg mixture to the rice and mix well. Stir in the flour mixture. Divide the rice mixture into 2 equal portions and place on 2 lightly oiled baking sheets. Spread each evenly with moistened fingers into a 10-inch square about 1/4 inch thick. Cover with oiled parchment paper. Cover the baking sheet and parchment with plastic wrap and chill for 4 to 24 hours. Divide the rice into 2-inch rice cakes. Heat 1 tablespoon of the peanut oil in a frying pan. Add the rice cakes and cook for 3 to 4 minutes on each side or until light brown, adding more peanut oil as needed. Remove the rice cakes to drain on paper towels.

For the tuna, mix the pineapple juice, soy sauce, brown sugar, garlic and ginger in a large sealable plastic bag. Add the tuna and seal the bag. Marinate in the refrigerator for 2 hours. Mix the peppercorns, anise seeds, nigella seeds, black sesame seeds and white sesame seeds together. Spread in an 8×8-inch rimmed dish. Drain the tuna, discarding the marinade. Roll each tuna log in the seed mixture until well coated. Wrap each log in plastic wrap, pressing the seeds firmly into the log. Chill for 1 hour. Heat 1/3 cup of the peanut oil in a medium frying pan over medium-high heat. Remove the tuna from the plastic wrap and sear 2 logs in the hot oil for 45 seconds per side. Remove the logs from the oil to paper towels to drain. Repeat with the remaining peanut oil and tuna logs.

For the salsa, combine the pineapple, onion, mint, grated ginger, minced ginger, peppercorns and salt in a nonreactive bowl and stir gently to mix. Let stand for 30 minutes before serving.

To serve, cut the tuna logs into 1/2-inch slices. Place each slice on a rice patty and top with 1/2 teaspoon of the salsa.

♡ To make heart healthy, sauté the tuna logs in 2 tablespoons peanut oil in a nonstick sauté pan coated with nonstick cooking spray. Serve on little Asian spoons instead of the rice patties.

Note: The tuna may be cut into a 2×2×2-inch triangular log 6 inches long.

Makes 4 dozen appetizers

PEAR WITH SMOKED TROUT

1/2 cup crème fraîche
1/2 teaspoon honey mustard
Salt and pepper to taste
4 pears, cut into wedges

1/3 pound smoked trout, cut into pieces

GARNISH
Fresh chives

Combine the crème fraîche, honey mustard, salt and pepper in a bowl and mix well. Spread a thin layer of the crème fraîche mixture on each pear wedge and top with a piece of smoked trout. Garnish with fresh chives.

Makes 16 appetizers

SUMMER SPRING ROLLS ♡ 𝕞

DIPPING SAUCE
3 tablespoons sugar
3 tablespoons fresh lime juice
2 tablespoons chopped fresh cilantro

5 tablespoons Asian fish sauce
1 1/2 teaspoons chili garlic sauce
Pinch of crushed red pepper flakes

SUMMER ROLLS
4 ounces cellophane rice noodles
1 cup shredded carrots
2/3 cup bean sprouts
1/4 cup chopped fresh cilantro
1/4 cup chopped fresh mint

1/4 cup finely chopped scallions
6 spring roll rice wrappers
6 medium shrimp, cooked and split
  into halves

For the sauce, whisk the sugar, lime juice, cilantro, fish sauce, garlic sauce and red pepper flakes in a small bowl. Chill, covered, until ready to serve.

For the summer rolls, cook the noodles using the package directions. Drain and rinse in cold water. Cut the noodles into 2-inch pieces. Combine the noodles, carrots, bean sprouts, cilantro, mint and scallions in a large bowl and toss to mix. Soak 1 rice wrapper at a time in a bowl of hot water until soft and remove to a towel. Place about 1/4 cup of the noodle mixture in the center of each wrapper and place 1 shrimp half on top. Fold the sides over and roll tightly. (You may make ahead up to this point and cover with a moist paper towel to prevent drying out.)

To serve, cut each roll-up diagonally into halves and serve with the sauce.

Note: Rice noodles and rice wrappers are available in Asian markets and some specialty food stores.

Serves 6

Belgian Endive Spears with Duck & Apricot

1/3 pound magret duck breast
3/4 cup moo shu duck marinade
2 2/3 tablespoons walnut oil
3/4 tablespoon red wine vinegar
3/4 tablespoon minced fresh ginger
2 tablespoons soy sauce
1/3 teaspoon minced garlic
2 tablespoons honey
1 1/3 tablespoons walnut pieces, toasted and coarsely chopped
1 1/3 tablespoons julienned dried apricots
2 tablespoons julienned water chestnuts
2 tablespoons julienned red bell pepper
1 1/3 tablespoons leek half moons (see Note)
3/4 tablespoon minced red onion
32 Belgium endive spears (about 3 or 4 nice size heads)

Remove the skin from the duck. Place the skinned duck and marinade in a sealable plastic bag and seal. Marinate in the refrigerator for 1 hour. Preheat the grill. Drain the duck, discarding the marinade. Place on a grill rack and grill until medium-rare or to the desired degree of doneness. Chill in the refrigerator and julienne.

Whisk the walnut oil, vinegar, ginger, soy sauce, garlic and honey in a bowl. Toss with the julienned duck, walnuts, apricots, water chestnuts, bell pepper, leek and red onion in a large bowl. Trim the endive spears to make uniform in size. Trim a small strip off the back of each spear so it will sit somewhat flat. Spoon 2 teaspoons of the duck mixture into each spear. Arrange on a complementing platter or tray and serve immediately.

Note: To cut the leek into half-moons, split the leek lengthwise into halves and then cut straight across the leek using the white and light green sections of the leek.

Makes 32 appetizers

PORK DUMPLINGS WITH CHEF VAL'S GINGER SOY DIPPING SAUCE

DUMPLINGS

10 to 12 large Napa cabbage leaves, cut into 1-inch pieces
1 tablespoon grated fresh ginger
3 green onions, finely chopped
2 tablespoons finely chopped cilantro
1/2 teaspoon fine sea salt
1/4 teaspoon freshly ground white pepper

1 1/2 tablespoons dark soy sauce
1 tablespoon rice wine
1 tablespoon sesame oil
2 teaspoons cornstarch
8 ounces ground pork
24 wonton wrappers
2 tablespoons peanut oil

CHEF VAL'S GINGER SOY DIPPING SAUCE

1/2 cup light soy sauce
1/4 cup rice vinegar
1/4 cup water
2 teaspoons toasted sesame oil
1 1/2 teaspoons sugar

1 tablespoon grated fresh ginger
1 teaspoon finely chopped garlic
1/2 teaspoon red pepper flakes, or to taste
1 tablespoon chopped fresh cilantro
2 scallions, green part only, thinly sliced

For the dumplings, pulse the cabbage in a food processor 4 or 5 times to coarsely chop. Place the cabbage on a clean dry dish towel. Gather the sides of the towel and squeeze out as much of the water as possible. (You should have 2 1/2 cups of chopped cabbage.) Combine the ginger, green onions, cilantro, sea salt, white pepper, soy sauce, rice wine, sesame oil and cornstarch in a large bowl and mix well. Add the ground pork and mix well. Stir in the cabbage. Place 1 tablespoon of the pork mixture in the center of each wrapper. Fold in half and pinch the top center edge to seal. On the edge facing you, make a series of 3 pleats on each side, pinching to seal as you go along. Pull the ends to form a crescent shape and tap the dumpling on the work surface to give it a flat "seat" that will brown nicely. (You may make ahead up to this point and freeze on a tray. When frozen, remove to a sealable plastic bag and store in the freezer for up to 4 weeks. Do not thaw before frying.)

Heat a nonstick sauté pan over medium-high heat and add the peanut oil. Arrange the dumplings in the skillet in a spiral fashion with the potstickers slightly touching each other. Fry for 1 to 2 minutes or until the bottoms are lightly brown. Add enough water to cover the dumplings half way. Bring to a boil and reduce the heat. Simmer, covered, for 7 minutes or until the liquid has been absorbed. Uncover and increase the heat to high. Continue to cook until any remaining liquid evaporates and the bottoms are brown and crisp.

For the sauce, combine the soy sauce, rice vinegar, water, sesame oil, sugar, ginger, garlic, red pepper flakes, cilantro and scallions in a small non-reactive bowl and mix well. Cover and chill for up to 2 weeks.

To serve, dip the hot dumplings in the sauce.

♡ To make heart healthy, substitute ground turkey for 1/2 of the ground pork.

Note: Won ton wrappers are available in the refrigerator section of most grocery stores.

Makes 2 dozen dumplings

Sesame Chicken Skewers

2 pounds boneless skinless chicken, cut
   into bite-size pieces
2 tablespoons rice wine vinegar
2 tablespoons dark Asian sesame oil
1 tablespoon chopped garlic
2 tablespoons soy sauce
1/4 cup black sesame seeds
1/4 cup white sesame seeds
2 tablespoons cornstarch
3 tablespoons all-purpose flour

Peanut oil for browning
Snow peas
3/4 cup mayonnaise
1 tablespoon rice wine vinegar
2 tablespoons chili paste with garlic
1 tablespoon soy sauce
1 tablespoon sesame oil
1 tablespoon minced fresh ginger
1 tablespoon sugar
1/2 red bell pepper

Place the chicken in a sealable plastic bag. Mix the rice wine vinegar, sesame oil, garlic and soy sauce in a small bowl. Pour over the chicken and seal the bag. Marinate in the refrigerator for 24 hours. (You may make ahead up to the point.) Mix the sesame seeds, cornstarch and flour together. Drain the chicken, discarding the marinade. Dredge the chicken in the sesame seed mixture and place on a tray. Let stand for 10 minutes. Heat a 1/4 inch of peanut oil in a sauté pan. Add the chicken in batches without crowding the pan and cook until the chicken is brown on all sides. Remove to paper towels to drain. Steam the snow peas for 1 minute. Wrap 1 snow pea around each piece of chicken and secure with a wooden pick.

Combine the mayonnaise, rice wine vinegar, chili paste with garlic, soy sauce, sesame oil, ginger and sugar in a bowl and mix well. Chill, covered, in the refrigerator until ready to serve. Spoon into the red bell pepper half just before serving. Serve the chicken with the dip.

Serves 6

Wasabi Mussels

3 pounds farm-raised mussels, cleaned
   and debearded
1 yellow or white onion, sliced
10 black peppercorns
1 carrot, sliced
1 rib celery, sliced
Handful of fresh Italian parsley

Kosher salt
2 cups water
1/2 cup mayonnaise
1 teaspoon fresh lemon juice
Zest from 1 lemon
2 teaspoons wasabi powder, or 1 tablespoon
   prepared wasabi, or to taste

Combine the mussels, onion, peppercorns, carrot, celery, parsley, kosher salt and water in a large stockpot and bring to a rapid boil. Cover and cook for 4 minutes or until the mussels open. Remove from the heat to cool.

Combine the mayonnaise, lemon juice, lemon zest and wasabi powder in a bowl and mix well. Remove the mussels from the shells, reserving the shells. Add the mussels to the mayonnaise mixture and mix well. Store, covered, in the refrigerator until ready to serve. Preheat the oven to 200 degrees. Place the best reserved unbroken mussel shell halves on a baking sheet and bake for 5 minutes or until dry. To serve, place the individual mussels on the half shells with a wooden pick in each and arrange on a tray spread with kosher or rock salt.

Serves 8

Rosemary Grilled Scallops & Shrimp 🍴

1 1/2 pounds sea scallops
30 large rosemary sprigs
6 ounces prosiutto, thinly sliced
1 1/2 pounds medium to large uncooked shrimp, peeled and deveined
6 tablespoons extra-virgin olive oil
6 tablespoons fresh lemon juice
Salt and pepper to taste

Rinse the scallops in water to remove the grit and sand. Remove the leaves from the bottom 2 inches of the rosemary sprigs, reserving the leaves and sprigs. Cut the prosciutto into 1×3-inch strips. Wrap a prosciutto strip around each scallop and each shrimp. Skewer a reserved rosemary sprig through 1 scallop and 1 shrimp. Repeat with the remaining rosemary sprigs, scallops and shrimp. Arrange each skewer in a shallow glass dish and drizzle with the olive oil and lemon juice. Sprinkle with the reserved rosemary leaves, salt and pepper and marinate for 30 minutes.

Preheat the grill. Place the skewers on a grill rack brushed with oil. Grill for 2 minutes per side or until the shrimp turn pink and the scallops are tender.

Note: When cooking scallops, be careful not to overcook. Similar to squid, scallops should be cooked either for a few minutes or for a long period of time. Anything in between will create a tough and rubbery texture.

Makes 30 appetizers

Tequila Fire Shrimp 🍴

1/2 cup garlic oil or olive oil
1/4 cup tequila
1/4 teaspoon cayenne pepper, or more for a spicier taste
2 garlic cloves, minced
1/2 cup Asian hot chili sauce (preferable Sriracha brand)
2 pounds large shrimp, peeled and deveined

Mix the garlic oil, tequila, cayenne pepper, garlic and hot chili sauce together and pour into a sealable plastic bag. Add the shrimp and seal the bag. Marinate in the refrigerator for 2 hours, or if a spicier taste is desired, marinate for 8 to 12 hours.

Preheat the grill. Drain the shrimp, reserving the marinade. Thread the shrimp on long metal skewers and place on a grill rack. Grill for 2 to 3 minutes per side or until the shrimp turn pink, basting frequently with the reserved marinade. Remove the shrimp from the skewers and place on a serving platter.

Note: Sriracha Hot Chili Sauce can be found in the Asian food section at Whole Foods.

Photograph for this recipe is on page 146.

Serves 6

Raw Seafood Bar

For a unique display, use a clean new concrete birdbath filled with ice to serve your raw seafood bar. It makes for a wonderful conversation piece and can be easily assembled and placed either on a table or stand on its own.

QUANTITY	SEAFOOD TYPE	CONDIMENT
2 dozen	Oysters-Bluepoint	Mignonette Sauce (below)
2 pounds	16- to 20-count shrimp	2 cups cocktail sauce
2 dozen	Crab Claws	1 cup horseradish sauce
2 dozen	Clams on the half shell	4 lemons

Mignonette Sauce

1 tablespoon coarsely ground white or black peppercorns, or to taste
1/2 cup white or red wine vinegar
2 tablespoons finely chopped shallots or sweet onions
Salt to taste

Combine the ground peppercorns, vinegar, shallots and salt in a bowl and mix well. Chill, covered, until ready to serve. Serve with chilled oysters or clams on the half shell.

Makes about 1/2 cup

This photograph is sponsored by Weichert Realtors, Hoey Group, Avalon, New Jersey, www.wrhoeygroup.com.

It's a good idea to hire helpers to serve and clean up. Check with local high schools and colleges for servers. Have them arrive well in advance of your party to brief them about your expectations before they begin serving your guests. Offer your guests wine, beer, or a signature cocktail like a Spring Fling (page 95), Beer Margarita (page 92), or Adult Watermelon Lemonade (page 96). Also, be sure to provide non-alcoholic options like flavored sparkling waters for your guests.

Remember to space out your bar area from stationary food displays so that traffic jams are avoided. Count on serving about six hors d'oeuvre per person per hour if you are not serving an entire meal. Make sure you offer a wide array of food options including vegetarian nibbles, fish, cheese, and meat. You should offer an assortment of both hot and room temperature hors d'oeuvre served at your party.

CANDY BACON DATES

These are always a big hit. Their simplicity makes them easy to prepare for the host, but absolutely delicious for the guest.

12 slices bacon
24 mejool dates
24 blanched whole almonds

Preheat the oven to 350 degrees. Cut each bacon slice into halves crosswise. Cook in a skillet until partially cooked through. Remove to paper towels to drain. Split each date and stuff with a blanched almond. Wrap each with a partially cooked bacon half and secure with a wooden pick. Place on a wire rack in a shallow baking pan. Bake for 30 minutes or until the bacon is crisp. Serve immediately. (You may assemble ahead, store in the refrigerator and then bake prior to serving.)

Makes 2 dozen appetizers

PAPAYA, CANTALOUPE & HONEYDEW SKEWERS WITH FRESH MINT & PROSCIUTTO

1/2 cup fine-quality olive oil
1/3 cup packed fresh basil leaves
1 shallot, cut into quarters
1 small cantaloupe
1 honeydew melon
3 papayas
6 thin slices prosciutto, cut into halves and gathered into a ruffle
1/3 cup fresh mint leaves
Freshly ground pepper to taste

GARNISHES
Fresh basil leaves
Fresh mint leaves

Pulse the olive oil, basil and shallot in a food processor until finely chopped. Cut the fruit into 1-inch pieces or scoop into bite-size balls with a small melon baller. Alternate the melon pieces with papaya, prosciutto and mint until six 8-inch wooden skewers are 3/4 filled. (You may make 2 hours ahead up to this point and store, covered, in the refrigerator. Bring to room temperature before serving.) Arrange the skewers on a serving platter. Drizzle with the olive oil mixture and sprinkle with freshly ground pepper. Garnish with fresh basil and mint leaves.

Makes 6 appetizers

PROSCIUTTO, GOAT CHEESE & FRESH FIG ROLL-UPS

8 ounces thinly sliced prosciutto
6 ounces soft mild goat cheese, at room temperature
1 1/2 teaspoons pepper
3 fresh figs, trimmed and cut into halves lengthwise
12 arugula leaves

Lay 2 slices of the prosciutto on a work surface and spread with some of the goat cheese. Sprinkle with pepper and layer with 1 fig half and 2 arugula leaves. Roll up and secure with a wooden pick. Repeat 5 more times with the remaining ingredients.

Note: For a great salad, arrange the roll-ups on a bed of mixed greens or arugula on individual salad plates and drizzle with high quality olive oil and fresh lemon juice. You can even make them into sophisticated sandwiches.

Makes 6 appetizers

PROSCIUTTO-WRAPPED ASPARAGUS SPEARS

24 thin asparagus stalks
12 slices prosciutto, cut into halves lengthwise (about 1/3 pound)
1/2 cup honey mustard
1/2 cup boursin cheese
1 tablespoon fine-quality olive oil
Freshly ground pepper to taste

GARNISH
1 lemon, sliced

Trim the bottom 2 inches off of each asparagus stalk. Place in a large pot of boiling water and boil for 4 minutes or until fork tender. Drain and place in an ice water bath to stop the cooking process. Let stand until cool.

Arrange the prosciutto halves on a work surface. Spread each half with 1 scant teaspoon honey mustard and 1 scant teaspoon boursin cheese. Wrap the prosciutto slice tightly around the middle of an asparagus spear so that the tip shows. Repeat 23 more times with the remaining asparagus. (Keep any remaining honey mustard or boursin cheese for another use.)

Arrange the wrapped asparagus spears in a tight circle on a serving tray. Drizzle with the olive oil and season with the pepper just before serving. Garnish with lemon slices in the center. (You may serve at room temperature and make several hours ahead.)

Makes 2 dozen appetizers

FINGERLING POTATOES WITH CAVIAR

25 fingerling potatoes
Salt and pepper to taste
2 cups sour cream or crème fraîche
1 small jar red or black caviar

GARNISH
Sprigs of fresh dill

Preheat the oven to 375 degrees. Line a baking sheet with foil and spray with nonstick cooking spray.

Scrub the potatoes and cut into 1-inch slices so the potatoes can stand upright. Arrange the potatoes on the prepared baking sheet and season with salt and pepper. Bake for 40 minutes or until tender. Remove from the oven to cool.

Arrange the potatoes in rows on a small platter. Place a dollop of sour cream on each potato and top with caviar. Garnish with sprigs of fresh dill. Serve immediately.

Makes 25 appetizers

CAVIAR

The Caspian Sea's icy waters are regarded as the best breeding ground of sturgeon, one of the world's most ancient species, producing ninety-five percent of the world's caviar. France has laws regulating that only processed roe of the female Caspian sturgeon can be called "caviar." The main types of caviar are Beluga, Osetra, and Sevruga, which are all equal in quality and are considered the ultimate in gourmet caviars. For a true splurge, try the Fingerling Potatoes with some Russian caviar. For domestic caviar choices, the American sturgeon or salmon roe work nicely and are a more value-conscious choice.

Many people consider caviar a true decadence, and to some people caviar represents a celebration of life, like Champagne. So cheers!

Red Pepper Gougères

I large red bell pepper, stemmed, seeded
    and cut into I-inch pieces
1/2 cup water
3 large garlic cloves, very finely chopped
6 tablespoons unsalted butter, cut into
    pieces
1/2 teaspoon salt

1/4 teaspoon freshly ground pepper
I cup all-purpose flour
4 eggs
1/2 cup (2 ounces) freshly grated
    pecorino Romano cheese
4 thin slices prosciutto, finely chopped

Preheat the oven to 425 degrees. Cover baking sheets with foil and spray with nonstick cooking spray. Process the bell pepper, water and garlic in a food processor for 2 minutes or until puréed. Strain the purée by pressing through a fine sieve over a measuring cup, extracting as much of the liquid as possible. (You should have about I cup of the pepper juice.) Discard the solids.

Combine the pepper juice, butter, salt and pepper in a medium saucepan and bring to a boil over medium-high heat. Add the flour all at once and stir with a large wooden spoon until the mixture pulls from the side of the pan and forms a ball. Scrape the dough into a mixing bowl. Add the eggs I at a time, beating well after each addition. Beat in the cheese and prosciutto. Drop by rounded teaspoonfuls I inch apart on the prepared baking sheets. Bake on the upper and middle oven racks for 22 minutes or until puffed and light brown, shifting the baking sheets from the top rack to the bottom rack halfway through baking. Serve hot, warm or at room temperature. (You may make ahead and store in an airtight container.)

Makes 3 dozen appetizers

Updated "Pigs in a Blanket"

3 (8-count) cans crescent rolls
I (12-ounce) package fully cooked chorizo
15 ounces manchego cheese
24 pitted medium green olives

Preheat the oven to 375 degrees. Unroll the crescent roll dough and separate into 24 triangles. Cut the sausage into twenty-four 1/4-inch slices. Cut the cheese into twenty-four 1/4-inch chunks. Place I slice sausage, I chunk of cheese and I green olive in the middle of each dough triangle. Bring up the dough to enclose the filling and form into a roughly shaped ball. Place on a baking sheet lined with Silpat. Bake for 12 to 16 minutes or until golden brown. Serve warm or at room temperature.

Note: For smaller appetizers to serve 48, cut all of the ingredients into halves for smaller pieces and reduce the baking time.

Makes 2 dozen appetizers

WARM EXOTIC MUSHROOM SPREAD WITH CROSTINI ♡ ⛁

CROSTINI
32 (1/2-inch-thick) slices baguette

I tablespoon truffle oil or olive oil

MUSHROOM SPREAD
I tablespoon olive oil
1/2 cup finely chopped shallots
2 garlic cloves, minced
2 cups sliced portobello mushrooms
2 cups sliced shiitake mushrooms
2 cups sliced button mushrooms
2 cups sliced oyster or trumpet
   mushrooms

I cup Madeira
1/3 cup chopped fresh Italian parsley
I teaspoon fresh thyme
I teaspoon salt
1/2 teaspoon freshly ground pepper
1/3 cup reduced-fat sour cream
I 1/2 teaspoons balsamic vinegar
I tablespoon chopped fresh Italian parsley

For the crostini, preheat the broiler. Place the bread slices in a single layer on a large baking sheet and brush evenly with the truffle oil. Broil for I minute or until light brown. (You may make up to 3 days in advance and store in a sealable plastic bag at room temperature.)

For the mushroom spread, heat the olive oil in a large skillet over medium-high heat. Add the shallots and garlic and sauté for 2 minutes. Add the sliced mushrooms and sauté for 8 minutes or until tender. Add the wine, 1/3 cup parsley, thyme, salt and pepper and bring to a boil. Boil for 15 minutes or until the liquid is almost evaporated. Remove from the heat and stir in the sour cream and vinegar. Spoon into a serving bowl and sprinkle with I tablespoon parsley. (You may make the spread I day ahead and chill in the refrigerator. Reheat in the microwave for a few minutes just before serving.) Serve the hot spread with the crostini.

Note: You may adjust the varieties of mushrooms in this recipe based upon your preference and availability.

Serves 16

Apple & Gorgonzola Bruschetta 🏛

1/2 cup crumbled Gorgonzola cheese
2 tablespoons butter, softened
1 to 2 tablespoons brandy or cognac
1/8 teaspoon pepper
12 (1/2-inch-thick) slices diagonal-cut French bread
3 garlic cloves, cut into halves
2 Granny Smith apples, cut into 12 (1/4-inch-thick) slices

Preheat the grill. Combine the cheese, butter, brandy and pepper in a bowl and mix well.

Place the bread slices on a grill rack and grill for 2 minutes or until light brown. (You may also toast the bread in the oven.)

Lightly rub the cut side of the garlic over 1 side of the bread to flavor. Spread 2 teaspoons of the cheese mixture over each slice and top with an apple slice.

Serves 12

Pumpkin Parmesan Toasts with Herb Pesto

1 loaf whole wheat bread
1/2 cup (2 ounces) freshly grated
   Parmesan cheese
1 cup fresh flat-leaf parsley leaves
1 cup loosely packed fresh cilantro
1/2 cup olive oil
2 tablespoons chopped fresh dill sprigs
1/3 cup walnuts
1/2 teaspoon cayenne pepper

1/2 teaspoon cumin
Kosher salt and freshly ground black
   pepper to taste
1 cup (4 ounces) freshly grated Parmesan
   cheese
1 cup canned unsweetened pumpkin purée
1/2 teaspoon cumin
2 tablespoons freshly grated Parmesan
   cheese

Preheat the oven to 400 degrees. Trim the crusts from the bread. Cut each bread slice twice to form 3 rectangles. Place on a baking sheet and bake for 12 minutes or until light brown. Remove from the oven to cool.

Pulse 1/2 cup Parmesan cheese, the parsley, cilantro, olive oil, dill and walnuts in a food processor until minced. Add the cayenne pepper, 1/2 teaspoon cumin, the kosher salt and black pepper and mix well.

Combine 1 cup Parmesan cheese, the pumpkin purée and 1/2 teaspoon cumin in a medium bowl and mix well. Season with kosher salt and black pepper.

Preheat the broiler. Spread each toast rectangle with 1 heaping teaspoon of the pesto and top with 1 1/2 heaping teaspoons of the pumpkin mixture. Arrange on a baking sheet and sprinkle with 2 tablespoons Parmesan cheese. Broil for 1 to 2 minutes or until light brown on top. Serve warm.

Serves 20

Sun-Dried Tomato & Brie Toasts 🎋

I (10-ounce) wheel Brie cheese
I French baguette
I (7-ounce) jar oil-pack sun-dried
  tomatoes, drained

$^1/_3$ cup olive oil
2 large garlic cloves, minced
$^1/_3$ cup pine nuts
3 tablespoons chopped fresh basil

Cut the rind from the cheese and discard. Cover the cheese and chill in the refrigerator. Cut the bread into slices $^3/_4$ inch thick. Place in a sealable plastic bag and store at room temperature. Pulse the sun-dried tomatoes in a food processor until almost puréed. Pour into a small bowl and chill in the refrigerator. (You may make I day ahead up to this point.)

Preheat the oven to 325 degrees. Arrange the bread on a baking sheet. Mix the olive oil and garlic in a small bowl and lightly brush over the bread. Bake for 5 minutes or until heated through. Remove from the oven and maintain the oven temperature.

Cut the cheese into slices $^1/_8$ inch thick. Spread I teaspoon of the tomato purée over each bread slice and top each with a slice of cheese. Bake for 2 minutes. Remove from the oven and sprinkle with the pine nuts. Bake for 5 minutes longer or until the cheese melts. Arrange on a serving platter and sprinkle with the basil.

Serves 8

Summertime Vegetable Caponata 🎋

I garlic clove
I cup olive oil
I bay leaf
Sliced celery to taste
I cup quartered mushrooms
I cup quartered onions
I cup bite-size carrots pieces
I cup bite-size cauliflower florets
I cup bite-size eggplant pieces

I cup bite-size green bell pepper pieces
I$^1/_2$ cups ketchup
I cup wine vinegar
2 tablespoons sugar
I tablespoon Dijon mustard
Salt and pepper to taste
12 large seedless green olives
12 black olives
Crusty French baguette slices

Sauté the garlic in the olive oil in a skillet for 5 minutes and discard the garlic. Add the bay leaf, celery, mushrooms, onions, carrots, cauliflower, eggplant and bell pepper and cook for 20 to 25 minutes or until tender crisp. Stir in the ketchup, vinegar, sugar, Dijon mustard, salt and pepper and cook for 5 to 6 minutes longer. Stir in the olives and remove from the heat to cool. Discard the bay leaf. Spoon into a bowl and chill for 2 to 5 days to enhance the flavor. Serve with baguette slices.

Note: You may add any amount of the vegetables to suit your individual taste.

Serves 10

FIG & WALNUT TAPENADE

1 cup stemmed Calimyrna figs
1/2 cup water
1/4 cup chopped pitted kalamata olives
2 tablespoons extra-virgin olive oil
1 tablespoon balsamic vinegar

2 tablespoons chopped drained capers
1 tablespoon chopped fresh thyme
3/4 cup walnuts, toasted and chopped
10 ounces fresh goat cheese, cut into
    1/2-inch slices

GARNISHES
Sprig of fresh thyme

Walnut halves

Chop the figs into 1/4-inch pieces. Combine the figs and water in a heavy medium saucepan. Simmer over medium heat or until the water evaporates and the figs are soft. (If the figs are not soft after the water evaporates, add additional water and continue to cook until the figs are soft.) Combine the fig mixture, olives, olive oil, vinegar, capers and chopped thyme in a medium bowl and mix well. (You may cover and chill for up to 3 days at this point. Return to room temperature before proceeding.) Stir in 3/4 cup walnuts.

To serve, arrange the cheese in an overlapping circle on a serving platter. Spoon the tapenade in the center and garnish with a sprig of fresh thyme and walnut halves. Serve with assorted crackers and breads.

Serves 20

ROASTED PEPPER & ARTICHOKE TAPENADE

1 (7-ounce) jar roasted red bell peppers,
    drained and coarsely chopped
1 (6-ounce) jar marinated artichoke
    hearts, drained and coarsely chopped
1/4 cup kalamata olives, pitted and
    chopped
1/2 cup fresh cilantro, minced

1/2 cup (2 ounces) freshly grated
    Parmesan cheese
1/3 cup olive oil
1/4 cup drained capers
2 garlic cloves, minced
1 tablespoon fresh lemon juice
Salt and pepper to taste

Pulse the bell peppers, artichoke hearts, olives, cilantro, Parmesan cheese, olive oil, capers, garlic and lemon juice in a food processor until well blended and finely chopped. Spoon into a serving bowl and season with salt and pepper. Serve with crostini (below) or crackers. (You may make 1 day ahead and store, covered, in the refrigerator.)

Serves 8

CROSTINI

*Cut a French baguette into slices and brush with olive oil.
Place on a baking sheet and broil until light brown on
both sides. Do not toast all of the way through.*

AVOCADO SHRIMP TOSTADAS

SHRIMP

1/4 cup minced onion
1/4 cup minced fresh parsley
I garlic clove, crushed
I teaspoon coriander
I teaspoon dry mustard
1/2 teaspoon cumin

1/2 teaspoon salt
Freshly ground pepper to taste
2 tablespoons lime juice
1/4 cup vegetable oil
12 medium shrimp, cooked, peeled and
  cut lengthwise into halves

GUACAMOLE

2 ripe Hass avocadoes, coarsely chopped
1/2 white onion, chopped
I medium to large fresh tomato, chopped
I jalapeño chile, coarsely chopped
  (include the seeds and veins)

I tablespoon coarsely chopped
  fresh cilantro
1/2 teaspoon kosher salt

ASSEMBLY

24 thick tortilla chips
I jar high-quality purchased salsa

I cup (4 ounces) shredded Monterey
  Jack cheese

For the shrimp, mix the onion, parsley, garlic, coriander, dry mustard, cumin, salt, pepper, lime juice and oil in a sealable plastic bag. Add the shrimp. Seal the bag and toss to coat. Marinate in the refrigerator for 8 to 12 hours. (You may make ahead up to this point.)

For the guacamole, lightly mash the avocadoes with a fork in a bowl. Add the onion, tomato, jalapeño chile, cilantro and kosher salt and mix well.

To assemble and serve, preheat the broiler. Spread I scant tablespoon of the guacamole on each chip. Top with a marinated shrimp, a scant teaspoon of salsa and a generous pinch of cheese. Place on a baking sheet and broil for I minute or until the cheese melts, watching carefully to prevent burning. Serve immediately.

Serves 12

GRILLED PIZZETTAS

1 package pizza dough
2 garlic cloves, crushed
Olive oil

SUN-DRIED TOMATO AND BASIL PIZZETTAS
Chopped oil-pack sun-dried tomatoes to taste
Chopped or torn fresh basil to taste
2 cups (8 ounces) shredded mozzarella cheese

FETA PIZZETTAS
1 jar of olive tapenade
Crumbled feta cheese to taste

CHEESE PIZZETTAS
Herbs de Provence or favorite pizza herbs to taste
2 cups (8 ounces) shredded mozzarella cheese
Freshly grated Parmesan cheese to taste

Preheat the grill to medium. Spray the grill rack with nonstick cooking spray. Divide the pizza dough into 4 equal portions and stretch into rounds. Place on the prepared grill rack and grill for 2 to 3 minutes or until the pizza rounds begin to puff up. Turn and grill for 1 minute. Remove to a baking sheet with the brown side facing up. (You may make a few hours in advance up to this point and wrap the cooled rounds in foil.)

Reduce the grill temperature to low. Mix the garlic and olive oil in a bowl and brush over the pizza rounds. Top with the ingredients to make Sun-Dried Tomato and Basil Pizzettas, Feta Pizzettas or Cheese Pizzettas, or top with any combination of ingredients to come up with your own special pizzettas. Return to the grill rack and grill for 4 minutes, closing the grill lid during the last minute to melt the cheese. Serve immediately.

Note: Olive tapenade can be found in the specialty food section of the supermarket. Pizza dough is available at Ardmore Farmers Market and your local supermarket.

Serves 4

Savory Fresh Herb Cheesecake

Pastry
1 cup all-purpose flour
1/2 cup (1 stick) butter, chilled
1/2 teaspoon salt

1 egg yolk
2 1/2 teaspoons finely grated lemon zest

Filling
16 ounces cream cheese
8 ounces goat cheese
3 tablespoons all-purpose flour
4 eggs
1 1/2 teaspoons salt
1 teaspoon pepper
2 tablespoons Dijon mustard
1 teaspoon Tabasco sauce

2 tablespoons lemon juice
3 garlic cloves, minced
1 large yellow onion, finely chopped
1/3 cup fresh flat-leaf parsley, chopped
1 tablespoon chopped fresh chives
1 tablespoon chopped fresh thyme
1 tablespoon chopped fresh chervil
   (optional)

Garnish
Fresh herbs

For the pastry, process the flour, butter, salt, egg yolk and lemon zest in a food processor until the mixture resembles cornmeal. Remove the dough and knead lightly. Shape into a ball and wrap in plastic wrap. Chill in the refrigerator for 1 hour. (You may make the dough a day ahead up to this point.) Press about 1/3 of the dough in the bottom of an 8-inch springform pan. Press the remaining dough around the side. Store in the freezer while preparing the filling.

For the filling, beat the cream cheese and goat cheese at medium speed in a mixing bowl until smooth. Add the flour and 1 of the eggs and beat until smooth. Add the remaining eggs 1 at a time, beating well after each addition. Add the salt, pepper, Dijon mustard, Tabasco sauce, lemon juice, garlic and onion and mix well. Add the parsley, chives, thyme and chervil and mix until evenly distributed throughout the batter.

To assemble, preheat the oven to 400 degrees. Pour the filling into the pastry-lined pan and bake for 10 minutes. Reduce the oven temperature to 325 degrees. Bake for 40 to 50 minutes or until the top is brown. Let stand for 1 hour before serving. Garnish with fresh herbs. Serve with chutney or salsa.

Note: The cheesecake is best served at room temperature, but it may also be served chilled.

Serves 8

Amuse-Bouche

"Amusement of the mouth," or appetizer.

TUSCAN CHEESE TORTA 🏛

CRUST
1/2 cup pine nuts
I cup finely ground all-natural
   wheat crackers

1/4 teaspoon fine crystal sea salt
1/4 teaspoon freshly ground pepper
I tablespoon unsalted butter, melted

PESTO FILLING
3 garlic cloves
1/2 cup pine nuts
2/3 cup freshly grated Parmigiano-
   Reggiano

1/2 teaspoon fine crystal sea salt
1/2 teaspoon freshly ground pepper
3 cups loosely packed fresh basil leaves
2/3 cup extra-virgin olive oil

CHEESE FILLING AND ASSEMBLY
Generous 1/2 teaspoon fine crystal sea salt
20 ounces cream cheese, softened
1/2 cup mascarpone cheese
3 eggs

1/4 teaspoon freshly ground pepper
I pound fresh figs
1/2 cup fig preserves, finely chopped
I 1/2 tablespoons white wine vinegar

GARNISH
Sprig of fresh basil

For the crust, place the oven rack in the middle of the oven and preheat the oven to 350 degrees. Butter a 10-inch springform pan. Place the pine nuts on a rimmed baking sheet and bake for 5 minutes or until toasted and golden brown. Remove the pine nuts to cool. Reduce the oven temperature to 325 degrees. Process the cooled pine nuts in a food processor until finely ground. Combine the processed pine nuts, crackers, salt, pepper and cooled butter in a large bowl and stir with a fork to combine. Press into the prepared springform pan. Bake for 10 minutes or until golden brown. Remove from the oven and cool on a wire rack. Maintain the oven temperature.

For the pesto filling, process the garlic in a food processor until just finely chopped. Add the pine nuts, Parmigiano-Reggiano, salt, pepper and basil and process until finely chopped. Add the oil in a fine stream, processing constantly until blended but not smooth. Measure I 1/4 cups of the pesto, reserving any remaining for another purpose.

For the cheese filling and assembly, reserve a pinch of the salt. Combine the cream cheese, mascarpone cheese, eggs, remaining salt and pepper in a medium bowl and beat until the mixture is smooth and creamy. Remove the fig stems and cut 1/2 of the figs into rings 1/4 inch thick. Pour 1/2 of the cheese filling into the baked crust. Spoon I 1/4 cups pesto over the cheese mixture, spreading evenly. Cover the pesto layer with the sliced figs. Pour the remaining cheese filling over the figs, spreading evenly. Bake on the middle oven rack for 50 to 60 minutes or until the top is set and golden brown. Remove from the oven to a wire rack to cool completely. Cover loosely and chill for 8 to 12 hours. (You may make up to 2 days ahead at this point.)

To serve, combine the fig preserves and vinegar in a small saucepan and bring to a simmer over medium heat. Remove from the heat to cool. Add the reserved pinch of salt and mix well. Slice the remaining figs into rings 1/8 inch thick. Run a knife around the edge of the chilled torta and remove the side of the pan. Spread the fig preserve mixture around the top, leaving a 1/2-inch border uncovered around the edge. Arrange the fig slices around the outside top of the torta, touching but not overlapping. Garnish the middle with a sprig of fresh basil. Serve at room temperature with lightly toasted baguette slices.

Serves 8 to 10

Goat Cheese Torta with Homemade Pita Chips

Torta
2 tablespoons high-quality
   olive oil
2 garlic cloves, crushed
1 (10-ounce) log goat cheese,
   such as Montrachet
1/2 cup kalamata olives, pitted

1/2 cup oil-pack sun-dried
   tomatoes
1/2 to 1 cup fresh basil leaves,
   torn
2 tablespoons pine nuts

Pita Chips
1 (6-count) package pita bread
Olive oil to taste

Salt and pepper to taste

For the torta, spread the olive oil on a platter. Spread the garlic in the olive oil and press the goat cheese into the middle of the mixture. Layer the olives, sun-dried tomatoes and basil over the goat cheese. Sprinkle with the pine nuts.

For the pita chips, preheat the oven to 350 degrees. Cut the pita bread into bite-size triangles and place on a baking sheet. Drizzle with olive oil and sprinkle with salt and pepper. Bake for 10 minutes or until crisp. (You may store the pita chips in an airtight container for several days.) Serve the torta at room temperature with the pita chips.

Note: You may adjust the amount of olives, sun-dried tomatoes, basil and pine nuts to suit your taste.

Serves 8

Cannellini Bean Dip

1 (15-ounce) can cannellini
   beans, drained
2 tablespoons fresh lemon juice
1 1/2 tablespoons extra-virgin
   olive oil
1 garlic clove
3/4 teaspoon cumin

Salt and pepper to taste
1 tablespoon chopped fresh mint
1 tablespoon chopped fresh dill
1 teaspoon grated lemon zest

Garnishes
Fresh mint and dill

Purée the beans, lemon juice, olive oil, garlic and cumin in a food processor. Season with salt and pepper and spoon into a small serving bowl. Mix the mint, dill and lemon zest in a small bowl and sprinkle over the dip. Chill, covered, for 24 hours to enhance the flavor. Serve with pita points, crudites or on French bread slices garnished with fresh mint and dill.

Serves 8

Spicy Gorgonzola Spread with Roasted Red Peppers 🚂

1 pound Gorgonzola cheese, crumbled
1²/₃ cups chopped roasted red bell peppers
1 tablespoon chopped fresh rosemary
2 scallions, minced
2 tablespoons sour cream
1 teaspoon sugar
1¹/₂ teaspoons Tabasco sauce
Crusty French bread slices

Purée the cheese, bell peppers, rosemary, scallions, sour cream, sugar and Tabasco sauce in a food processor. Spoon into a serving bowl. Chill, covered, until thick. Serve on the bread slices. You may top each slice with scallions, prosciutto, anchovies, additional roasted red bell peppers or crumbled cooked bacon.

Makes 2 cups

Greek Six-Layer Dip 🚂

1 (15-ounce) can white beans, drained and rinsed
1 tablespoon minced garlic, or to taste
¹/₄ cup extra-virgin olive oil
1 tablespoon lemon juice
1 teaspoon dried dill
1 teaspoon oregano
¹/₈ teaspoon salt
1 tablespoon red wine vinegar
1 teaspoon Dijon mustard
¹/₂ large red onion, finely chopped
¹/₂ large zucchini, shredded
2 ounces feta cheese, crumbled
¹/₂ cup chopped tomato
1 (2-ounce) can sliced black olives, drained

Process the beans, garlic, olive oil, lemon juice, dill, oregano, salt, vinegar and mustard in a blender or food processor until processed to a somewhat smooth texture. Spread in the bottom of a serving dish. Sprinkle the onion, zucchini, feta cheese, tomato and olives in even layers over the bean mixture. Chill, covered, until ready to serve. Serve with chips.

Serves 8

Nectarine Guacamole ♡ ▥

2 nectarines or peaches, coarsely chopped
3 green onions, sliced
1 small avocado, chopped
3 tablespoons snipped fresh cilantro
3 tablespoons lime juice or orange juice
1 large garlic clove, minced
1/4 teaspoon salt

Combine the nectarines, green onions, avocado, cilantro, lime juice, garlic and salt in a medium bowl and toss to mix. Chill, covered, for up to 3 hours.

For a complete heart-healthy appetizer, serve with toasted pita chips or vegetable or corn chips prepared with canola oil.

Makes about 1 3/4 cups

Spicy Cashews ▥

2 cups canola oil
8 ounces whole raw cashews
1/4 teaspoon salt
1/4 to 1/2 teaspoon freshly ground pepper

Place a large sieve over a bowl large enough to hold the oil and place near the stove. Line 2 dinner plates with paper towels and place near the stove.

Pour the oil into a deep 8-inch frying pan and heat over medium heat until hot but not smoking. Add the cashews carefully. Stir-fry until the cashews are red-gold in color. Remove immediately from the heat and pour the cashews and oil into the sieve. Lift the sieve and carefully shake off the excess oil. Spread the cashews on 1 of the prepared plates, stirring to help absorb the oil. Immediately sprinkle with the salt and pepper and stir to mix. Spread the cashews over the remaining prepared plate to absorb any additional oil. Serve warm or cool.

Makes 8 ounces

Brunch & Beverages

Pancetta & Gorgonzola Strata 🏛

8 ounces challah or panettone
10 ounces thinly sliced pancetta (Italian bacon)
$1^1/4$ cups heavy cream
$1^1/4$ cups milk
1 teaspoon salt
2 teaspoons Tabasco sauce or hot sauce
5 eggs
10 ounces Gorgonzola cheese, crumbled
12 ounces St. André cheese, crumbled
$^1/4$ cup chopped fresh rosemary

Preheat the oven to 350 degrees. Cut the bread into 1-inch slices and place on a baking sheet. Bake until the bread is lightly toasted on each side. Cut the pancetta into eight $^1/2$-inch slices. Sauté the pancetta in a heavy skillet over medium-low heat for 10 minutes or until crisp. Remove to paper towels to drain. Whisk the cream, milk, salt, Tabasco sauce and eggs in a medium bowl.

Layer 4 slices of the bread in a buttered $2^1/2$-quart soufflé dish. Layer the Gorgonzola cheese, St. André cheese, rosemary and pancetta evenly $^1/2$ at a time over the bread. Pour the egg mixture over the layers. Let stand, covered, for 30 minutes.

Preheat the oven to 350 degrees. Uncover the strata and bake for 40 minutes or until golden brown and bubbly. Remove from the oven and let stand for 10 minutes before serving.

Serves 8

Maple Pecan Bacon

$^1/2$ cup pure maple syrup
1 pound sliced bacon
$1^1/2$ cups pecans, finely chopped

Preheat the oven to 400 degrees. Pour the syrup into a shallow dish. Dip the bacon into the syrup 1 slice at a time, letting the excess drip off. Arrange the bacon on a rack in a broiler pan. Sprinkle with the pecans and press into place if necessary to adhere. Bake for 30 minutes or until cooked through, watching carefully to prevent overbrowning.

Serves 6 to 8

OEUFS À LA CHIMAY

12 jumbo hard-cooked eggs, cut into
   halves lengthwise
1/4 cup (1/2 stick) unsalted butter
6 ounces wild mushroom mix
   (such as shiitake, oyster and baby
   bella), finely chopped
2 sprigs of fresh thyme
2 whole shallots, finely chopped
Salt and pepper to taste
3 tablespoons unsalted butter
1 tablespoon finely chopped shallots

3 tablespoons all-purpose flour
3 1/3 cups milk
2 sprigs of fresh thyme
1 bay leaf
Ground nutmeg to taste
2/3 cup finely grated Parmigiano-Reggiano
2/3 cup grated Gruyère cheese
1 1/3 cups milk
3 tablespoons chopped fresh
   flat-leaf parsley

Separate the egg yolks from the egg whites. Rub the yolks through a coarse mesh sieve into a mixing bowl. Melt 1/4 cup butter in a large sauté pan over medium-high heat. Add the mushroom mix and 2 sprigs of thyme and sauté until the liquid evaporates. Add 2 shallots, finely chopped, and season with salt and pepper. Sauté for 1 minute and remove from the heat. Remove the sprigs of thyme. Add the yolks to the mushroom mixture and mix gently to blend.

Melt 3 tablespoons butter in a large sauté pan over medium-high heat. Add 1 tablespoon shallots and sauté until translucent. Add the flour and cook for 2 minutes or until the mixture is buttery yellow in color, stirring constantly with a wooden spoon. Do not allow to brown. Whisk in 3 1/3 cups milk and reduce the heat to low. Add 2 sprigs of thyme, the bay leaf, nutmeg, salt and pepper. Cook for 30 minutes or until thickened, stirring constantly. Strain the sauce through a sieve into another saucepan, discarding the solids. Mix the Parmigiano-Reggiano cheese and Gruyère cheese together. Return the white sauce to low heat and gradually add the cheese mixture and 1 1/3 cups milk, stirring constantly to blend. Cook until the cheese melts and the sauce is smooth, stirring constantly. Remove from the heat. (You may make the cheese sauce up to 2 days in advance. After the cheese has been incorporated and the sauce is smooth, remove from the heat and allow to cool for 15 minutes, stirring every few minutes to prevent a skin from forming. Apply a layer of plastic wrap directly onto the surface of the sauce and chill, covered, until ready to use. Reheat gently over very low heat, stirring constantly to prevent sticking or scorching.)

Preheat the oven to 325 degrees. Add 1/2 cup of the cheese sauce to the yolk mixture and mix well. Continue to add additional cheese sauce until a moist stuffing consistency is achieved. Place a generous mound of the stuffing in each of the egg whites and arrange into rows in a buttered 9×13-inch baking dish. Cover the eggs with the remaining cheese sauce. Bake for 15 to 20 minutes or until the sauce is bubbling. Remove from the oven and sprinkle with the parsley.

Serves 12

Fiesta Frittata

I tablespoon olive oil
3 garlic cloves, minced
I large red onion, sliced
2 red bell peppers, julienned
I yellow bell pepper, julienned
I tablespoon olive oil
2 yellow squash, thinly sliced
2 zucchini, thinly sliced
I tablespoon olive oil
8 ounces sliced mushrooms
6 eggs
$1/4$ cup heavy cream
$2^{1}/2$ to 3 teaspoons salt
2 teaspoons freshly ground pepper
2 cups cubed high-quality Artisan
    white bread
8 ounces cream cheese, cut into cubes
2 cups (8 ounces) coarsely shredded Gruyère cheese

Preheat the oven to 325 degrees. Heat I tablespoon olive oil in a large skillet. Add the garlic, onion and bell peppers and sauté until tender. Remove from the skillet to drain on paper towels.

Heat I tablespoon olive oil in a large skillet. Add the squash and zucchini and sauté until tender. Remove from the skillet to drain on paper towels.

Heat I tablespoon olive oil in a large skillet. Add the mushrooms and sauté until tender. Remove from the skillet to drain on paper towels.

Whisk the eggs, cream, salt and pepper in a large bowl. Stir in the sautéed bell pepper mixture, squash mixture, mushrooms, $1/2$ of the bread cubes, the cream cheese and Gruyère cheese.

Press the remaining bread cubes in a lightly greased 10-inch springform pan and place on a baking sheet. Pour the vegetable mixture into the prepared pan. Bake for I hour, covering with foil after 45 minutes to prevent excess browning. Serve warm.

Serves 8

CHRISTMAS MORNING BREAD PUDDING

1 cup packed light brown sugar
1/2 cup (1 stick) butter, melted
1 teaspoon ground cinnamon
3 Granny Smith apples, peeled and thinly sliced
1/2 cup dried cranberries or raisins
1 loaf soft French or Italian bread, cut into 1-inch-thick slices
6 eggs
1 1/2 cups milk
1 tablespoon vanilla extract
2 teaspoons ground cinnamon

Combine the brown sugar, butter and 1 teaspoon cinnamon in a mixing bowl. Add the apples and cranberries and toss to coat. Spread evenly in a 9×13-inch baking pan. Layer the bread slices over the apple mixture.

Beat the eggs, milk, vanilla and 2 teaspoons cinnamon with a fork in a bowl until blended. Pour over the bread to completely soak. Cover and chill for up to 24 hours.

Preheat the oven to 375 degrees. Bake, covered, for 40 minutes. Uncover and bake until light brown.

Serves 8

MIXED BERRIES WITH LEMON CREAM

8 ounces cream cheese, softened
1/3 cup confectioners' sugar
2 teaspoons finely grated lemon zest
2 tablespoons fresh lemon juice
1 cup heavy whipping cream
2 pints fresh strawberries, sliced
1 pint blueberries
1 pint raspberries
1 pint blackberries

Process the cream cheese, confectioners' sugar, lemon zest and lemon juice in a food processor until smooth. Chill for 1 hour or longer.

To serve, whip the whipping cream in a mixing bowl until stiff peaks form. Place assorted berries in parfait glasses and top each with a dollop of the lemon cream and a dollop of the whipped cream. (You may use your favorite berries or the freshest berries available in your market.)

Serves 8

Walnut Pear Sour Cream Cake

1 cup broken walnuts
1/2 cup packed light brown sugar
1/2 teaspoon ground cinnamon
1/2 teaspoon cardamom
1/4 cup (1/2 stick) butter
1/3 cup all-purpose flour
2 pears, peeled and sliced (about 2 cups)
2 teaspoons fresh lemon juice
1 3/4 cups all-purpose flour
3/4 teaspoon baking powder
1/2 teaspoon baking soda
1/2 teaspoon salt
1/2 cup (1 stick) unsalted butter, softened
1 cup granulated sugar
1 teaspoon vanilla extract
2 eggs
1 cup sour cream

Preheat the oven to 350 degrees. Mix 1 cup walnuts, the brown sugar, 1/2 teaspoon cinnamon and the cardamom in a bowl. Cut 1/4 cup butter into 1/3 cup flour in a bowl to resemble coarse crumbs. Stir in 3/4 cup of the walnut mixture to form the topping. Toss the pears with the lemon juice in a bowl.

Mix 1 3/4 cups flour, the baking powder, baking soda and salt together. Beat 1/2 cup butter in a large mixing bowl for 30 seconds. Add the granulated sugar and vanilla and beat well. Add the eggs 1 at a time, beating well after each addition. Add the flour mixture and sour cream alternately, beating at low speed after each addition until combined. Spread 2/3 of the batter into a greased 9-inch springform pan. Sprinkle with the remaining walnut mixture. Layer the pears over the walnut mixture. Spread the remaining batter over the pears and sprinkle with the topping.

Bake for 55 to 60 minutes or until a wooden pick inserted in the center comes out clean. Run a knife around the edge of the pan to loosen and remove the side of the pan. Cool the coffee cake on a wire rack for at least 1 hour.

Note: For a nuttier top, sprinkle with an additional 1/2 cup chopped walnuts after the cake has baked for 10 minutes.

Serves 10

Pumpkin Muffins with Ginger Walnut Streusel

Streusel Topping

1 cup coarsely chopped walnuts

1 cup packed dark brown sugar

1/2 cup all-purpose flour

1 cup finely chopped crystallized ginger

2 teaspoons ground cinnamon

1/4 cup (1/2 stick) unsalted butter, melted

Muffins

3 cups all-purpose unbleached flour

1 tablespoon baking powder

2 teaspoons baking soda

1 teaspoon salt

1 tablespoon ground cinnamon

2 teaspoons ginger

1 teaspoon ground allspice

2 cups canned pumpkin purée

2 cups firmly packed light brown sugar

1 cup canola oil

4 eggs

For the topping, toss the walnuts, brown sugar, flour, ginger, cinnamon and butter with a fork in a bowl until blended and crumbly.

For the muffins, preheat the oven to 400 degrees. Line 24 muffin cups with foil or paper liners. Sift the flour, baking powder, baking soda, salt, cinnamon, ginger and allspice together. Combine the pumpkin purée, brown sugar, oil and eggs in a mixing bowl and beat until smooth. Add the flour mixture and stir until combined, being careful not to overmix. Fill each muffin cup 1/2 full. Sprinkle each with 1 heaping tablespoon of the topping. Bake on the middle oven rack for 15 to 17 minutes or until a wooden pick inserted in the center of the muffins comes out clean. Remove the muffins to cool on a wire rack. (You may make the muffins ahead and freeze.)

Makes 2 dozen

Popover Pancake

1/2 cup all-purpose flour

1/2 cup milk

2 eggs, lightly beaten

Pinch of nutmeg

1/4 cup (1/2 stick) butter

2 tablespoons confectioners' sugar

Juice of 1/2 lemon

Preheat the oven to 425 degrees. Combine the flour, milk, eggs and nutmeg in a bowl and mix well. Melt the butter in an ovenproof 12-inch skillet and add the batter. Bake for 15 to 20 minutes or until golden brown. Remove from the oven and sprinkle with confectioners' sugar. Return to the oven and bake briefly to melt the confectioners' sugar. Remove from the oven and sprinkle with the lemon juice.

Serves 2

Fluffy Sour Cream Pancakes

1 1/4 cups all-purpose flour
2 teaspoons sugar
1 teaspoon baking powder
1/2 teaspoon salt
1 1/2 cups sour cream
1 teaspoon baking soda
3 egg yolks
3 tablespoons butter, softened
3 egg whites, stiffly beaten

Whisk the flour, sugar, baking powder and salt together. Mix the sour cream and baking soda in a bowl. Beat the egg yolks in a mixing bowl until light and fluffy. Add to the sour cream mixture and mix well. Stir in the flour mixture. Add the butter and beat at medium speed for 30 seconds. Fold in the egg whites. Pour 1/4 cup of the batter at a time onto a hot, lightly greased griddle. Cook until brown on both sides, turning once. You may sprinkle berries or chocolate chips on the unbaked side of each pancake once spooned onto the griddle.

Makes 1 dozen pancakes

Apricot Ginger Butter

2 cups coarsely chopped dried apricots (8 ounces)
1 cup orange juice
1/2 cup water
1 1/2 tablespoons chopped fresh ginger
2 tablespoons honey
2 tablespoons sugar

Bring the apricots, orange juice, water and ginger to a boil in a heavy saucepan and reduce the heat. Simmer, covered, for 20 minutes or until the liquid is reduced by 1/2 and the apricots are very tender, stirring frequently. Purée the mixture in a food processor until smooth. Add the honey and sugar and mix well. (You may make and store in the refrigerator 1 week ahead.) Serve with scones and muffins.

Makes about 1 cup

Peach Bellini

Named for the painter Giovanni Bellini, this famous cocktail was created at Harry's Bar in Venice, Italy. When fresh white peaches are unavailable, a commercial peach purée may be substituted.

Simple Syrup

I cup sugar

1/2 cup water

Bellini

3 to 4 very ripe white peaches,
  peeled and pitted

4 ounces Prosecco
  (Italian sparkling wine)

For the simple syrup, bring the sugar and water to a boil in a saucepan and cook until all of the sugar crystals are dissolved. Remove from the heat to cool.

For the bellini, process the peaches in a food processor until puréed. Mix I ounce of the puréed peaches and I ounce of the simple syrup in a bowl. Strain the mixture through coarse cheesecloth into a bowl, discarding the solids. Chill in the refrigerator.

To serve, pour I ounce of the nectar into a Champagne flute and top with the Prosecco.

Serves I

Caipirinha

8 limes, cut into 8 wedges each
  and halved

I bottle cachaça
  (Brazilian sugarcane brandy)

I cup sugar

Ice cubes

Place the lime wedges and sugar in the bottom of a pitcher. Crush and mash the limes to release the oils and juice from the rind, using a muddler or the handle of a wooden spoon. Continue to crush and mash until the sugar begins to dissolve. Add the liquor and stir to combine. To serve, pour the cocktail into ice-filled lowball glasses. Do not remove the pieces of crushed lime.

Serves 6

Cranberry Kir Royale

1/2 cup frozen cranberry juice cocktail
  concentrate, thawed

2 cups chilled Champagne

Pour 2 tablespoons cranberry concentrate into each of 4 chilled Champagne glasses. Add 1/2 cup Champagne to each glass and serve.

Note: You may freeze fresh cranberries and drop a few in each glass as a garnish before serving.

Serves 4

The Best Margaritas

I (12-ounce) can frozen limeade
   concentrate, thawed
I limeade can tequila

$^1/2$ limeade can Grand Marnier
$^1/4$ limeade can fresh lime juice with zest
Water

Pour the limeade concentrate, tequila, Grand Marnier and lime juice in a 2-quart container. Fill the rest of the way with water and chill in the refrigerator. Serve over ice in salted-rim glasses. Ole!

Serves 16

Beer Margaritas

Juice of 2 limes
Margarita salt
2 Corona beers, chilled
$^1/2$ cup good quality tequila
$^1/2$ cup thawed frozen limeade concentrate

GARNISH
Lime wedges

Moisten the rim of 4 margarita glasses with the lime juice and press into salt to coat. Mix the beers, tequila and limeade concentrate in a pitcher. Pour into glasses and garnish each with a lime wedge.

Serves 4

Ginger Martinis

I (6- to 7-inch-long) piece of
   fresh ginger
2 cups vodka
I (12-ounce) bottle of nonalcoholic
   ginger beer
$1^1/2$ cups frozen passion fruit juice
   cocktail concentrate, thawed

GARNISHES
6 star anise
6 sprigs of fresh mint

Peel the ginger and cut lengthwise into slices $^1/4$ inch thick. Cut each slice lengthwise into $^1/4$ inch sticks to make at least 6. Combine the vodka, ginger beer and passion fruit juice cocktail concentrate in a pitcher. (You may make the ginger sticks and beverage ahead up to this point, covering each separately and chill until ready to serve.)

To serve, pour the beverage over ice in martini glasses. Garnish each with a ginger stick, star anise and sprig of mint.

Serves 6

Key Lime Martinis

Lime juice
Graham cracker crumbs
4 fresh Key lime wheels or regular lime wheels
2 cups cracked ice
4 ounces Rose's lime juice
4 ounces Ke Ke Beach Key lime cream liqueur
4 ounce Triple Sec
4 ounces Licor 43 liqueur (Spanish vanilla liqueur)
4 ounces half-and-half

Chill 4 martini glasses. Moisten the rim of each with lime juice and press about $1/4$ inch deep into graham cracker crumbs. Attach a Key lime wheel on the rim of each martini glass. Fill a metal cocktail shaker with the cracked ice. Place the top on the shaker and shake for 10 to 15 seconds. Add 4 ounces lime juice, the Key lime liqueur, Triple Sec, Licor 43 liqueur and half-and-half and shake for 15 seconds or until frothy. Strain into the prepared glasses and serve immediately.

Serves 4

Midori Champagne Cocktail

1 shot midori
Champagne

GARNISH
1 fresh raspberry

Pour the midori into a Champagne glass. Add enough Champagne to fill the glass and garnish with a fresh raspberry.

Serves 1

HONEY BRUNCH MIMOSAS

1 (6-ounce) can frozen lemonade concentrate, thawed
1/4 cup Grand Marnier or other orange-flavored liqueur
1/4 cup honey, warmed
1 bottle (750 milliliters) dry Champagne, chilled

GARNISH
Fresh strawberries

Combine the lemonade concentrate and Grand Marnier in a large pitcher. Add the honey and stir until dissolved. Stir in the Champagne just before serving. Pour into individual Champagne glasses and garnish with strawberries.

Serves 6

PIMM'S CUP

Pimm's No. 1 is a gin-based liqueur flavored with fruits, spices and herbs. Initially intended as a digestive tonic, Pimm's Cup was invented in the 1800s by James Pimm of England. This refreshing drink is a tradition for local horsemen gathering for carriage-driving events. During the Devon Carriage Marathon, antique horse-drawn vehicles travel a four-mile route starting with judging at St. David's Church and ending at the 108-year-old Devon Horse Show and Country Fairgrounds.

1 1/4 ounces Pimm's No. 1
3 ounces lemonade
Lemon-lime soda

GARNISH
1 cucumber, cut to resemble a pickle

Fill a 12-ounce glass with ice and pour in the Pimm's No. 1 and lemonade. Add enough lemon-lime soda to fill the glass and garnish with the cucumber.

Serves 1

Spring Flings

1 cup sugar
1 cup fresh mint leaves
3 lemons, thinly sliced into rounds
2 cucumbers, thinly sliced into rounds
2^1/$_2$ cups vodka
2 cups fresh lemon juice
2 cups (or more) club soda

GARNISHES
8 slices of mint
8 slices of cucumber
8 slices of lemon

Combine the sugar, mint leaves, lemon slices and cucumber slices in a pitcher and mix well. Pour in the vodka and lemon juice and let stand for 30 minutes. Stir the mixture until the sugar is dissolved and chill for 30 minutes. Stir in the club soda just before serving and pour over ice in glasses. Garnish each with a slice of mint, cucumber and lemon.

Serves 8

Springtime-tini

3 cups vodka
2^1/$_2$ cups Champagne
^{1}/$_2$ cup bottled sweet-and-sour mix
2 tablespoons Chambord
2 tablespoons fresh lime juice

Combine the vodka, Champagne, sweet-and-sour mix, Chambord and lime juice with ice cubes in a pitcher and stir to mix well. Strain into martini glasses to serve. (You may coat the rims of the martini glasses with superfine sugar.)

Serves 12

ADULT WATERMELON LEMONADE

2 cups water
2 cups vodka
2 cups fresh lemon juice
1 cup sugar
4 cups puréed seeded fresh watermelon

GARNISHES
Lemon rounds
Fresh mint leaves

Combine the water, vodka, lemon juice, sugar and watermelon purée in a pitcher and mix well. Chill in the refrigerator. Serve over ice and garnish with lemon rounds and mint leaves.

Serves 8

SUMMER SANGRIA

1 (750-milliliter) bottle white wine such
   as a lite chardonnay or zinfandel
1/2 cup peach schnapps
2 tablespoons Cointreau or other
   orange-flavored liqueur
2 tablespoons sugar
2 cinnamon sticks, broken into halves

1 lemon, sliced
1 orange, sliced
1 peach, cut into wedges
1 apple, cut into wedges
1 (10-ounce) bottle of club soda, chilled

Combine the wine, peach schnapps, Cointreau, sugar, cinnamon sticks, lemon slices, orange slices, peach wedges and apple wedges in a large pitcher and mix well. Let stand to allow the flavors to blend. Stir in the club soda just before serving. Pour into ice-filled glasses and serve.

Serves 6

FALL CIDER PUNCH

10 cups apple cider
5 cups club soda
2 1/2 cups brandy
1 1/4 cups orange-flavored liqueur
Ice cubes

GARNISHES
5 oranges, studded with whole cloves
5 apples, studded with whole cloves

Combine the apple cider, club soda, brandy and orange-flavored liqueur in a punch bowl and mix well. Just before serving, add ice cubes and garnish with the oranges and apples. Serve cold.

Serves 15 to 18

BRANDYWINE PUNCH

1 cup fresh lemon juice
$1/2$ cup orange juice
$1/2$ cup sugar
$1 1/2$ cups brandy
$1 1/2$ cups amontillado sherry
$1/4$ cup ruby port
$1/4$ cup Cointreau
2 (750-milliliter) bottles of Champagne, chilled
1 liter club soda, chilled
Ice cubes

GARNISHES
6 cinnamon sticks
Slices of fresh lemons
Slices of fresh oranges

Combine the lemon juice, orange juice and sugar in a large punch bowl and stir until the sugar dissolves. Add the brandy, sherry, port, Cointreau, Champagne and club soda and stir to blend. Add ice cubes and garnish with cinnamon sticks, sliced lemons and sliced oranges. Serve immediately.

Makes 1 gallon

"SPIRITUAL" FACTS:

That whiskey is the key by which many gain entrance into our prisons and almshouses.

That brandy brands the noses of all those who cannot govern their appetites.

That punch is the cause of many unfriendly punches.

That ale causes many ailings, while beer brings to the bier.

That wine causes many to take a winding way home.

That Champagne is the source of many real pains.

That gin slings have slewed more than slings of oil.

Chester County Cookery

Soups · Salads Side Dishes

HONEYDEW & WHITE WINE SOUP ♡ ⁙

8 cups diced chilled honeydew melon (about 1 large melon)
1 cup fruity white wine
3 tablespoons lime juice
1 tablespoon honey, or to taste
1/2 cup fresh raspberries

Process the honeydew melon, wine, lime juice and honey in a blender until puréed and frothy. Pour into an airtight container and chill for 1 to 6 hours. Before serving, stir the soup to redistribute any remaining foam. Ladle into large balloon wine glasses or martini glasses and scatter a few raspberries on top of each.

Serves 4

MANGO GAZPACHO SOUP ♡ ⁙

4 cups (1 quart) chopped plum tomatoes
2 green bell peppers, chopped
2 cucumbers, chopped
3/4 cup mango chunks
1/3 cup sugar
1/3 cup chopped fresh cilantro
4 cups (1 quart) low-sodium vegetable juice cocktail
1/4 cup red wine vinegar
1 teaspoon hot sauce
1 tablespoon extra-virgin olive oil

GARNISHES
Fat-free plain yogurt or nonfat sour cream
Sprigs of fresh cilantro

Process the tomatoes, bell peppers, cucumbers, mango chunks, sugar, cilantro, vegetable juice cocktail, vinegar, hot sauce and olive oil in a large food processor until the mixture is of a coarse consistency. Pour into an airtight container and chill until ready to serve. (You may store in the refrigerator for up to 2 days.)

Ladle into soup bowls and garnish each serving with a dollop of yogurt and a sprig of cilantro.

Serves 8 to 10

Mushroom Barley Soup ♡

2 garlic cloves, chopped
1 cup onion, finely chopped
1/4 cup sherry
2 1/2 cups sliced baby bella mushrooms
2 1/2 cups sliced button mushrooms
5 cups vegetable or chicken stock

1/2 cup barley
1 tablespoon tamari soy sauce
1 tablespoon dried dill
1 teaspoon tarragon
Freshly ground nutmeg to taste
Salt and freshly ground pepper to taste

Sauté the garlic and onion in the sherry in a stockpot over medium heat for a few minutes or until the onion softens. Add the mushrooms and sauté until the mushrooms are soft, adding some of the stock if necessary. Add the remaining stock and bring to a boil. Reduce the heat and add the barley. Simmer, covered, over medium heat for 1 hour. Season the soup with the tamari soy sauce, dill, tarragon, nutmeg, salt and pepper. Cook for a few minutes longer and ladle into soup bowls to serve.

Serves 10

Wild Mushroom Soup with Sherry

6 tablespoons butter, softened
2 cups sliced celery
1 cup sliced shallots
3/4 cup chopped onion
3 garlic cloves, minced
3 cups sliced stemmed fresh shiitake
  mushrooms (about 6 ounces)
3 cups sliced crimini mushrooms
  (about 6 ounces)
3 cups sliced oyster mushrooms
  (about 4 1/2 ounces)

1/2 cup dry white wine
1/2 cup dry sherry
2 tablespoons butter, softened
1/4 cup all-purpose flour
8 cups (2 quarts) chicken stock, or
  canned low-salt chicken broth
1/2 cup heavy cream
Salt and pepper to taste

Melt 6 tablespoons butter in a stockpot over medium-high heat. Add the celery, shallots, onion and garlic and sauté for 8 minutes or until the onion is translucent. Add the mushrooms and sauté for 4 minutes or until the mushrooms are beginning to soften. Add the white wine and sherry and boil for 6 minutes or until the liquid is reduced to a glaze consistency.

Mix 2 tablespoons butter and the flour in a small bowl to form a smooth paste. Add to the mushroom mixture and cook until the butter mixture melts and coats the vegetables, stirring constantly. Add the stock gradually, stirring constantly. Bring to a boil, stirring frequently. Reduce the heat to medium-low and simmer for 10 minutes or until the mushrooms are tender, stirring frequently. Stir in the cream and season with salt and pepper.

Purée the soup in batches in a blender or food processor and return to the stockpot. (You may make 1 day ahead up to this point. Cover and chill in the refrigerator. Reheat over medium-low heat before serving.) Ladle the soup into bowls and serve.

Serves 8 to 10

CURRIED PUMPKIN & SWEET POTATO SOUP

I teaspoon chopped fresh garlic
I cup finely chopped onion
$1^1/2$ teaspoons olive oil
$2^1/2$ cups low-sodium chicken stock
I large sweet potato, peeled and chopped
I cup mashed cooked pumpkin
$1^1/2$ teaspoons curry powder
$^1/2$ teaspoon chopped fresh cilantro
I tablespoon honey
$^1/2$ teaspoon ground ginger
Light cream

Sauté the garlic and onion in the olive oil in a stockpot until softened. Add the chicken stock, sweet potato, pumpkin, curry powder, cilantro, honey and ginger. Simmer, covered, for 40 minutes. Process in batches in a blender or food processor until smooth. (You may make ahead up to this point and store, covered, in the refrigerator.)

Return the puréed soup to the stockpot. Reheat slowly, adding enough light cream to achieve desired consistency. Ladle into soup bowls to serve.

♡ For a heart-healthy alternative, substitute fat-free evaporated milk for the light cream.

Serves 4

Chicken Salad with Roasted Asparagus & Toasted Almonds ♡

2¹/2 cups (1-inch-diagonally cut) asparagus pieces
2 teaspoons olive oil
Salt and pepper to taste
¹/4 cup fat-free mayonnaise
¹/4 cup low-fat yogurt
1 teaspoon curry powder
1 teaspoon fresh lemon juice
¹/4 teaspoon salt
¹/8 teaspoon pepper
2 cups chopped roasted skinless chicken breasts
¹/2 red bell pepper, sliced
¹/2 yellow bell pepper, sliced
¹/2 cup chopped fresh parsley
2 tablespoons sliced toasted almonds

Preheat the oven to 400 degrees. Place the asparagus on a baking sheet and drizzle with the olive oil and season with salt and pepper to taste. Bake for 15 minutes or until roasted, watching closely to prevent overbrowning. (You may also steam the asparagus until tender-crisp.)

Whisk the mayonnaise, yogurt, curry powder, lemon juice, ¹/4 teaspoon salt and ¹/8 teaspoon pepper in a large bowl. Add the asparagus, chicken, bell peppers, parsley and almonds and toss to coat.

Serves 4

Minted Chicken & Melon Salad

MINTY VINAIGRETTE
¹/4 cup fresh lemon juice
¹/2 cup chopped fresh mint
²/3 cup olive oil
2 tablespoons red wine vinegar
¹/2 teaspoon sugar
Salt and pepper to taste

SALAD
4 boneless skinless chicken breasts, grilled or poached
¹/2 Cranshaw or honeydew melon, cut into chunks
¹/2 cup crumbled feta cheese
1 cup grape tomatoes, cut into halves
Mint leaves from 5 sprigs of fresh mint
Mixed salad greens
Salt and pepper to taste
¹/2 cup toasted walnut halves

For the vinaigrette, cook the lemon juice and mint in a small saucepan over high heat for 1 minute or until the mint wilts. Remove from the heat and let steep for 10 minutes. Strain into a small bowl, discarding the mint. Whisk the olive oil, vinegar and sugar into the strained juice and season with salt and pepper.

For the salad, cut the chicken into thin slices. Combine the chicken, melon, feta cheese, tomatoes and mint leaves in a bowl and toss to mix. Add ¹/2 of the vinaigrette and toss gently to coat. Pour the remaining vinaigrette over the salad greens in a bowl and toss gently to coat. Season with salt and pepper. Divide the salad greens among 4 salad plates and spoon the chicken salad over the top. Sprinkle with the toasted walnuts.

Serves 4

Lobster & Papaya Salad ♡

1 (2¼-pound) lobster, cooked and shelled
4 cups mixed salad greens
1 avocado, sliced
1 papaya, seeded and sliced
1 tablespoon raspberry vinegar
2 tablespoons olive oil
Salt and pepper to taste

GARNISH
Sprigs of fresh dill

Cut the lobster into ¾-inch chunks. Divide the salad greens between 2 salad plates and arrange the avocado slices, papaya slices and lobster over the salad greens. Whisk the raspberry vinegar, olive oil, salt and pepper in a bowl and drizzle over each salad. Garnish with sprigs of fresh dill.

Serves 2

Spicy Shrimp & Black Bean Salad ♡ ▥

1 (15-ounce) can black beans, rinsed and drained
1 green bell pepper, chopped
½ cup chopped celery
½ cup chopped purple onion
2 tablespoons chopped fresh cilantro
1 or 2 jalapeño chiles, seeded, deveined and finely chopped
⅔ cup salsa
¼ cup fresh lime juice
2 tablespoons canola oil
2 tablespoons honey
¼ teaspoon salt
Lettuce leaves
2 pounds peeled cooked shrimp
Chopped fresh cilantro to taste

Combine the black beans, bell pepper, celery, onion, 2 tablespoons cilantro, jalapeño chiles, salsa, lime juice, canola oil, honey and salt in a bowl and toss gently to mix. Chill, covered, for 8 hours.

To serve, spoon the black bean mixture in the center of a lettuce-lined platter. Arrange the shrimp around the edge and sprinkle with chopped fresh cilantro to taste.

Serves 4

Shrimp Ceviche with Carrot, Orange & Fennel ♡ ⛲

LEMON OIL
1/2 cup canola oil
1/2 teaspoon turmeric

1 tablespoon finely grated fresh
   lemon zest

CARROT ORANGE SAUCE
4 cups (1 quart) fresh carrot juice
4 cups (1 quart) fresh orange juice
2 stalks fresh lemon grass (lower 6 inches
   only), thinly sliced crosswise

1 tablespoon minced fresh ginger
2 fresh Thai red chiles, minced (including
   seeds), or 2 dried red chiles, minced

SALAD
2 pounds (21- to 25-count) large shrimp,
   peeled and deveined
1/2 teaspoon salt, or to taste
2 carrots, cut into very thin matchsticks
3 navel oranges

1 fennel bulb, cut into halves lengthwise
1 small red onion, cut into halves lengthwise
1/2 cup fresh lime juice
1/4 cup (1-inch) fresh chives pieces
2 tablespoons finely chopped fresh mint

For the lemon oil, cook the canola oil, turmeric and lemon zest in a 1- to 2-quart saucepan over low heat for 5 minutes, stirring frequently. Pour into a small bowl and chill for 1 hour or longer. Pour through a fine-mesh sieve into another small bowl, discarding the solids. (You may make the lemon oil up to 1 day ahead and chill in the refrigerator. Strain after 1 to 2 hours of chilling, then cover.)

For the sauce, bring the carrot juice, orange juice, lemon grass, ginger and red chilies to a boil in a 4- to 6-quart saucepan. Boil for 30 to 40 minutes or until reduced to 2 cups, stirring occasionally. Pour through a medium-mesh sieve into a bowl, discarding the solids. Set the bowl in a larger bowl of ice and cold water to chill the sauce. (You may make the sauce 1 day ahead and chill, covered, in the refrigerator.)

For the salad, cook the shrimp in boiling salted water in a 4- to 6-quart stockpot for 1 to 2 minutes or until the shrimp just turn pink. Drain and place the shrimp in a large bowl of ice and cold water to cool. Drain the shrimp and cut into halves lengthwise. Place the shrimp in a bowl. Cover and chill in the refrigerator.

Heat 1/4 cup of the lemon oil in a heavy 10-inch skillet over medium-high heat until hot but not smoking. Add the carrots to the hot oil and sauté for 4 to 5 minutes or until just tender. Spread the carrots with the drippings from the skillet onto a platter and chill in the refrigerator.

Grate the zest from the oranges into a large bowl. Cut the remaining rind and white pith from the oranges with a sharp paring knife and discard. Cut the orange sections from the membranes and add to the zest. Cut the fennel and onion very thinly crosswise. Stir the carrots, fennel, onion, lime juice and remaining lemon oil into the orange mixture. Stir in the chives and mint just before serving.

To serve, mound the salad onto 8 serving plates and top with the shrimp. Drizzle about 3 tablespoons of the sauce around each mound and over the shrimp. Serve the remaining sauce on the side.

Note: A Japanese Benriner or other adjustable-blade slicer and a rasplike Microplane zester make preparation of this recipe easier. This equipment is available at Asian markets, some cookware shops, and Uwajimaya (800-889-1928).

Serves 8

ARUGULA & LEAFY GREENS WITH PARMESAN BOW TIES & BALSAMIC APPLE VINAIGRETTE

PARMESAN BOW TIES
1/4 cup (heaping) freshly grated
   Parmigiano-Reggiano cheese

BALSAMIC APPLE VINAIGRETTE
1/4 cup balsamic vinegar
1/2 cup white vinegar
1 cup canola oil
1/4 cup olive oil
1/2 teaspoon white pepper
1 1/2 teaspoons sea salt
1/2 teaspoon minced shallot
1/4 teaspoon minced garlic
1 green apple, peeled and chopped
1/4 cup finely chopped fresh parsley

SALAD
2 cups arugula
1 cup green leaf lettuce
2 teaspoons drained capers
12 red raspberries

For the bow ties, preheat the oven to 325 degrees. Line a baking sheet with parchment paper. Sprinkle about 2 teaspoons of the cheese onto the prepared baking sheet and spread into a 2-inch circle. Repeat with the remaining cheese to make 6 circles. Bake for 6 to 8 minutes or until golden brown. Pinch each circle at the center using cooking tongs while still hot to form bow tie shapes. Let stand until cool. (You may store in an airtight container for up to 2 days.)

For the vinaigrette, process the balsamic vinegar, white vinegar, canola oil, olive oil, white pepper, sea salt, shallot, garlic and apple in a food processor until blended. Chill, covered, for 8 to 12 hours. Stir in the parsley and adjust the seasonings to taste just before serving. (The vinaigrette makes enough to serve 20 to 24.)

For the salad, combine the arugula and green leaf lettuce in a salad bowl and toss to mix. Toss in enough vinaigrette to coat the salad greens and divide between 2 salad plates. Add 1 teaspoon capers, 6 red raspberries and 3 parmesan bow ties to each plate and serve immediately.

Serves 2

Salad with Mango Dressing ♥

3 mangoes
1/4 cup rice vinegar
3 tablespoons canola oil
2 tablespoons honey
I tablespoon chopped red onion
I teaspoon snipped fresh mint
I teaspoon snipped fresh chives

Pinch of cayenne pepper or black pepper
Salt to taste
I1/2 heads red leaf lettuce or mixed salad
    greens, torn into bite-size pieces
1/2 cup watercress leaves
3 tablespoons snipped fresh basil

Peel, pit and cut the mangoes into slices. Chop enough of the mango slices to measure 3/4 cup, reserving the remaining mango slices for the salad. Process 3/4 cup chopped mangoes, vinegar, canola oil, honey, onion, mint and chives in a blender until smooth. Season with the cayenne pepper and salt.

Toss the lettuce, watercress and basil in a salad bowl and place on individual salad plates. Arrange the reserved sliced mangoes over the lettuce and drizzle with the mango dressing.

Serves 8

Point-to-Point Salad with Spicy Cashews

Poppy Seed Dressing
1/4 onion, grated
1/2 cup sugar
1/2 cup vegetable oil

1/3 cup apple cider vinegar
I teaspoon dry mustard
I1/2 teaspoons poppy seeds

Salad
Romaine, Bibb lettuce, or
    red leaf lettuce, torn
Sliced strawberries

Cubed Brie cheese
1/2 cup Spicy Cashews (page 81)

For the dressing, mix the onion, sugar, 1/2 of the oil and a small amount of the vinegar in a bowl. Add the remaining oil and vinegar gradually, beating constantly. Stir in the dry mustard and poppy seeds. Chill until ready to serve.

For the salad, combine the lettuce, strawberries and cheese in a salad bowl and toss to mix. Add the dressing and toss to coat. Sprinkle with the Spicy Cashews.

Serves 8

Spinach Salad with Fried Blue Cheese

Fried Blue Cheese
8 ounces Roquefort or other blue cheese
1/4 cup all-purpose flour
2 eggs, lightly beaten
1/2 cup plain or Italian-seasoned bread crumbs
Vegetable oil for frying

Salad
1 garlic clove, cut into halves
1/4 teaspoon salt
2 tablespoons red wine vinegar
1 teaspoon Worcestershire sauce
6 tablespoons olive oil
1 pound fresh spinach, trimmed

For the fried blue cheese, freeze the cheese for at least 30 minutes to prevent crumbling. Cut the cheese into 3/4-inch cubes. Dredge the cheese in the flour, shaking off the excess. Coat thoroughly with the eggs and dredge in the bread crumbs. Heat 2 inches of vegetable oil in a saucepan. Fry the cheese cubes in batches for 45 to 60 seconds or until golden brown, removing with a slotted spoon to paper towels to drain.

For the salad, mash the garlic and salt in a large bowl to form a paste. Add the vinegar, Worcestershire sauce and olive oil and mix well. Add the spinach and toss to coat. Divide among 4 salad plates and top with the fried cheese cubes.

Serves 4

Roasted Pear & Blue Cheese Salad

Praline Pecans
2/3 cup pecans, coarsely chopped
1/2 teaspoon kosher salt
1/4 teaspoon cayenne pepper, or to taste
6 tablespoons sugar

Ancho Chile Vinaigrette
2 cups fresh orange juice
2 tablespoons red wine vinegar
2 tablespoons chopped red onion
2 teaspoons ancho chile powder
3/4 cup extra-virgin olive oil
1 tablespoon honey
Salt and pepper to taste

Salad
5 ripe Bosc pears, peeled and cut into halves
2 tablespoons vegetable oil
20 cups mixed salad greens, such as frisee, arugula, etc.
1 cup crumbled blue cheese

For the praline pecans, toss the pecans with the kosher salt and cayenne pepper in a small bowl. Place the sugar in a heavy dry skillet and cook over medium heat until the sugar starts to melt, stirring gently. Continue to cook until the sugar turns golden caramel in color, swirling the skillet frequently. Remove from the heat and stir in the pecan mixture. Pour onto a lightly oiled large baking sheet and spread evenly with a knife. Cool completely and crack into pieces. Store in an airtight container.

For the vinaigrette, boil the orange juice in a small saucepan for 12 to 13 minutes or until reduced to 1/2 cup. Process the orange juice, vinegar, onion and chile powder in a blender until smooth. Drizzle in the olive oil and honey in a fine stream, processing constantly. Season with salt and pepper.

For the salad, preheat the oven to 425 degrees. Place each pear half cut-side down on a baking sheet and drizzle with the oil. Roast for 15 minutes and brush with the accumulated juices. Roast for 13 to 15 minutes longer. Turn the pears and baste with the pan juices again. Roast for 10 minutes longer or until tender. Remove from the oven to cool. Cut into thirds lengthwise.

Toss the salad greens with 1/2 cup of the vinaigrette in a large bowl. Place on individual salad plates and top with the roasted pears. Sprinkle with the pecans and crumbled blue cheese. Drizzle with the remaining vinaigrette.

Note: Ancho chile powder is available from the coffee/spice stand in the back of the Lancaster County Farmers Market.

Serves 10

Apple Cherry Walnut Salad with Creamy Maple Dressing

Creamy Maple Dressing
1/4 cup mayonnaise
1/4 cup pure maple syrup
3 tablespoons Champagne or white wine vinegar
3 tablespoons Dijon mustard
1 garlic clove, minced
1/2 cup canola oil

Salad
2 Granny Smith apples, cut into 1/8-inch wedges
1 cup dried cherries
1/2 cup walnuts, coarsely chopped
3 ounces goat cheese, crumbled
Red leaf lettuce or mixed salad greens

For the dressing, whisk the mayonnaise, maple syrup, Champagne, Dijon mustard and garlic in a bowl. Add the canola oil gradually, whisking constantly. (You may make days ahead and store in the refrigerator.)

For the salad, combine the apples, dried cherries, walnuts, goat cheese and salad greens in a salad bowl and toss to mix. Add the salad dressing and toss to coat.

Serves 6 to 8

Fruit Salad Macerated with Framboise ♡

2 ripe mangoes, cut into bite-size pieces
1 pound strawberries, cut into quarters
2 kiwifruit, cut into half-moon slices
1 cup blueberries
1/2 cup sugar
Juice of 1 orange
2 tablespoons Framboise
2 to 3 teaspoons grated orange zest
1 tablespoon finely chopped fresh mint

Combine the mangoes, strawberries, kiwifruit and blueberries in a shallow serving bowl. Add the sugar, orange juice, Framboise, orange zest and fresh mint and stir gently to mix. Cover with plastic wrap and macerate in the refrigerator for 2 to 12 hours before serving.

Serves 8

APPLE SLAW

4$^{1}/_{2}$ cups thinly sliced red apples, such as McIntosh or Stayman
3 cups finely shredded green cabbage
1 fennel bulb, minced
1 cup crème fraîche
3 tablespoons lemon juice
1 tablespoon honey
$^{3}/_{4}$ teaspoon salt
$^{1}/_{8}$ teaspoon pepper
1 tablespoon poppy seeds

Combine the apples, cabbage, fennel, crème fraîche, lemon juice, honey, salt, pepper and poppy seeds in a large bowl and toss to mix. Cover and chill for 1 hour or longer before serving.

Serves 6 to 8

CITRUS ASPARAGUS SALAD

HONEY MUSTARD VINAIGRETTE
$^{1}/_{4}$ cup rice wine vinegar
2 tablespoons Dijon mustard
2 tablespoons honey
1 tablespoon finely chopped fresh tarragon
Salt and freshly ground pepper to taste
$^{3}/_{4}$ cup canola oil

SALAD
12 ounces asparagus, trimmed
1 orange
4 slices Serrano ham
$^{1}/_{3}$ cup caperberries
Salt and pepper to taste

For the vinaigrette, combine the rice wine vinegar, Dijon mustard, honey, tarragon, salt and pepper in a bowl and mix well. Whisk in the canola oil gradually.

For the salad, blanch the asparagus in boiling water for 3 minutes. Immediately submerge in ice water to stop the cooking process. Remove the asparagus to a bowl and add the vinaigrette. Cover and marinate in the refrigerator for 3 hours.

Grate the zest from the orange and reserve. Peel the orange and cut crosswise into thin slices. Drain the asparagus, discarding the marinade. Arrange the asparagus down the center of a serving platter. Arrange the orange slices around the asparagus, overlapping slightly. Ribbon the ham over the asparagus and sprinkle with the caperberries and reserved orange zest. Season with salt and pepper.

Serves 4

Summer Mint & Cucumber Salad ♡ ⛩

2 cucumbers
I teaspoon kosher salt
1/4 cup minced shallots
1/4 cup fresh mint leaves, chopped
1 1/2 tablespoons fresh lemon juice
I teaspoon grated lemon zest
Freshly ground pepper to taste

Peel the cucumbers and cut into halves lengthwise. Remove the seeds and cut crosswise into slices 1/4 inch thick. Place the cucumbers in a colander and set over a bowl. Sprinkle with the salt and let stand for 1 hour. Rinse the cucumbers under cold running water and pat dry. Combine the cucumbers, shallots, mint, lemon juice, lemon zest and pepper in a medium bowl and toss to mix. Cover and chill in the refrigerator for several hours for the flavors to blend. (You may make up to 12 hours before serving.)

Serves 8

Brazilian Potato Salad ⛩

2 pounds sweet potatoes
I tablespoon salt
1/2 cup drained and rinsed black beans
1/2 red onion, chopped
1/4 cup cilantro, chopped
1/2 cup mayonnaise
2 tablespoons olive oil
I teaspoon Dijon mustard
I teaspoon Worcestershire sauce
2 tablespoons red wine vinegar
1/2 teaspoon salt
1/2 teaspoon pepper

Scrub the sweet potatoes and cut off the ends. Place in a large saucepan and cover with water. Sprinkle with I tablespoon salt and cover. Bring to a gentle boil and boil for 20 to 30 minutes or until tender. Drain and let stand until the sweet potatoes are cool enough to handle. Peel the sweet potatoes and cut into cubes in a bowl. Add the black beans, onion and cilantro and toss to mix. Whisk the mayonnaise, olive oil, Dijon mustard, Worcestershire sauce, red wine vinegar, 1/2 teaspoon salt and pepper in a bowl. Pour over the warm sweet potato mixture and toss to coat. Cover and chill until ready to serve.

Serves 6 to 8

Tomato Napoleon with Fresh Tomato Dressing ﷼

TOMATO DRESSING
I cup olive oil
1/2 cup balsamic vinegar
3 garlic cloves, sliced
I tablespoon sugar
I teaspoon salt
I teaspoon pepper
4 large tomatoes, peeled and chopped
2 tablespoons fresh thyme leaves, or 4 sprigs of fresh thyme

SALAD
8 slices fresh mozzarella cheese
8 thick slices tomato
I teaspoon salt
I teaspoon pepper
Shredded fresh basil leaves to taste

For the dressing, whisk the olive oil, balsamic vinegar, garlic, sugar, salt and pepper in a bowl. Stir in the tomatoes and thyme. Cover and let stand at room temperature for I hour, stirring occasionally. Cover and chill for 8 hours before serving. (You may store in the refrigerator for up to 2 weeks.)

For the salad, pour 3/4 cup of the dressing over the cheese in a shallow dish. Cover and chill for I hour. Remove the cheese slices, reserving the dressing. Sprinkle the tomato slices with the salt and pepper. Place I tomato slice on each of 4 salad plates. Top each with I slice of cheese and some shredded basil. Repeat the layers with the remaining tomato slices, cheese slices and basil. Drizzle evenly with the reserved dressing. (You may assemble 2 hours ahead of time and store, covered, in the refrigerator.)

Serves 4

Asian Noodle Salad ♡ ▥

Asian Dressing
3/4 cup fresh lime juice (about 3 large limes)
1/3 cup hoisin sauce
1 1/2 tablespoons sugar
1 1/4 teaspoons crushed red pepper
4 garlic cloves, minced

Salad
6 ounces cellophane noodles
2 eggs, lightly beaten
2 tablespoons water
1/2 teaspoon salt
1 teaspoon olive oil
2 cups grated English cucumbers
2 cups grated carrots
6 tablespoons chopped dry roasted peanuts
1/4 cup chopped fresh cilantro
2/3 cup chopped fresh basil

For the dressing, whisk the lime juice, hoisin sauce, sugar, red pepper and garlic in a bowl.

For the salad, cook the cellophane noodles using the package directions. Do not overcook. Drain and rinse with cold water. Whisk the eggs, water and salt in a bowl. Heat 1/2 teaspoon of the olive oil in a skillet. Add 1/2 of the egg mixture and cook until fried and set. Remove to a cutting board and cut the fried egg into strips 1/2-inch wide and 4 inches long. Repeat with the remaining oil and egg mixture. Arrange the noodles, cucumbers, carrots and egg strips in separate piles on a serving platter for a beautiful presentation. Sprinkle with the peanuts, cilantro and basil. Drizzle with the dressing just before serving and toss to coat.

Serves 6

Spicy Thai Noodle Salad

Spicy Thai Dressing
3 garlic cloves
1 1/2 tablespoons minced fresh ginger
1/2 cup peanut butter
3 tablespoons rice vinegar
2 tablespoons chili garlic sauce
3 tablespoons soy sauce
Cayenne pepper to taste
1/2 cup (or less) sesame oil

Salad
12 ounces angel hair pasta or thin linguini
Salt to taste
1/4 cup sesame oil
1 cup julienned carrots
1 red bell pepper, julienned
1 small cucumber, julienned
8 green onion bulbs, chopped
1/2 cup chopped peanuts

Garnishes
8 green onion stems
Sprigs from 1 bunch of fresh cilantro
Julienned red bell pepper

For the dressing, combine the garlic, ginger, peanut butter, rice vinegar, chili garlic sauce, soy sauce and cayenne pepper in a food processor and pulse until blended. Add 1/2 of the sesame oil in a fine stream, processing constantly. The dressing should be thick enough to coat a spoon. If the dressing is too thick, add the remaining sesame oil and process to form the correct consistency.

For the salad, cook the pasta in boiling salted water in a large stockpot until al dente. Drain and place in a large bowl. Add the sesame oil and toss to coat. Pour the dressing over the pasta and toss to coat. Add the carrots, bell pepper, cucumber and green onion bulbs and toss to coat. Cover and chill until ready to serve. (You may make 1 day ahead up to this point.)

To serve, add the chopped peanuts and toss to mix. Garnish with the green onion stems, sprigs of cilantro and julienned bell pepper. You may serve the salad cool or at room temperature.

Serves 8

Summer Rice Salad

1 1/2 cups basmati rice
Juice of 1 lemon
4 ribs celery, sliced
1 cup chopped red onion
1/2 cup currants

1 cup olive oil
4 teaspoons Dijon mustard
Salt and pepper to taste
1/2 cup pecans
Chopped fresh parsley to taste

Cook the rice using the package directions and drain. Add the lemon juice, celery, red onion, currants, olive oil, Dijon mustard, salt and pepper and mix well. Cover and marinate in the refrigerator for 8 to 24 hours. Stir in the pecans and parsley just before serving.

Serves 8 to 10

Asparagus with Exotic Mushroom Sauce

2 bunches fresh asparagus, trimmed
Salt to taste
2 ounces shiitake mushrooms, sliced
2 ounces oyster mushrooms, sliced
1 tablespoon finely chopped shallots
1/4 teaspoon minced garlic
1 tablespoon olive oil
1/2 cup chicken stock

1/4 cup white wine
1/4 cup heavy cream
1/4 teaspoon finely chopped fresh
   Italian parsley
Pepper to taste

GARNISH
Chopped fresh chives

Cook the asparagus in boiling salted water in a saucepan for 2 to 3 minutes or until firm yet tender enough to pierce with a fork. Plunge immediately into ice water to stop the cooking process.

Sauté the shiitake mushrooms, oyster mushrooms, shallots and garlic in the olive oil in a sauté pan over medium heat until the liquid is evaporated. Add the chicken stock and wine, stirring to deglaze the pan and scrape up any brown bits. Cook over medium-high heat until the sauce is reduced by 1/4. Add the cream and cook until the sauce is reduced by 1/4. Season with the parsley, salt and pepper.

To serve, fan 4 to 6 stalks of asparagus on each serving plate. Spoon the mushroom sauce on the asparagus at the bottom of the stalks. Garnish with chopped chives.

Serves 6

Roasted Asparagus with Lemon Sage Butter

2 pounds thin asparagus, trimmed
1 tablespoon olive oil
1/2 teaspoon kosher salt
1/4 cup (1/2 stick) unsalted butter
35 fresh sage leaves

2 tablespoons fresh lemon juice
1 tablespoon lemon zest
1/4 teaspoon kosher salt
3/4 cup chopped toasted hazelnuts

Preheat the oven to 450 degrees. Toss the asparagus with the olive oil and 1/2 teaspoon kosher salt in a bowl. Arrange in a single layer on a baking sheet and bake for 5 minutes or until tender. (You may grill the asparagus if desired.)

Melt the butter over medium-low heat in a medium frying pan. Add the sage leaves and cook until the butter is light brown and the sage leaves are crispy, stirring constantly. Stir in the lemon juice, lemon zest and 1/4 teaspoon kosher salt.

To serve, arrange the asparagus on a warm serving platter and drizzle with the butter. Sprinkle with the toasted hazelnuts.

Serves 6 to 8

Photograph for this recipe is on page 142.

Crowd-Pleasing Beans

1 pound ground round or ground sirloin
1 large onion, chopped
1/2 bell pepper, finely chopped
1 (16-ounce) can pork and beans
1 (16-ounce) can lima beans or
  butter beans
1 (16-ounce) can light red kidney beans

1/2 cup packed brown sugar
1/2 cup ketchup
2 tablespoons mustard
2 tablespoons Worcestershire sauce
1 1/2 tablespoons chili powder
1 teaspoon salt
6 slices bacon, crisp-cooked and crumbled

Preheat the oven to 350 degrees. Brown the ground round with the onion and bell pepper in a skillet. Add the undrained beans, brown sugar, ketchup, mustard, Worcestershire sauce, chili powder and salt and mix well. Spoon into a 9×13-inch baking dish sprayed with nonstick cooking spray. Sprinkle with the bacon. Bake for 45 minutes.

Serves 10 to 12

French Green Beans with Pears & Parmesan

3 pounds haricots verts or other thin
  green beans
Salt to taste
6 tablespoons walnut oil
1/2 cup olive oil
6 tablespoons sherry wine vinegar
6 tablespoons chopped fresh chives
6 tablespoons chopped fresh parsley

6 tablespoons minced shallots
1 cup small fresh basil leaves
Pepper to taste
4 small firm ripe pears, peeled and cut
  into matchstick-size strips
1 cup chopped walnuts
3 ounces Parmesan cheese, shaved with
  a vegetable peeler

Cook the haricots verts in boiling salted water in a large saucepan for 6 minutes or until tender-crisp. Drain and rinse in cold water to stop the cooking process. Whisk the walnut oil, olive oil, sherry wine vinegar, chives, parsley and shallots in a large bowl. Add the haricots verts and basil and toss gently. Season with salt and pepper. (You may make 1 day ahead up to this point and chill in the refrigerator.)

To serve, add the pears and walnuts to the haricots verts mixture and toss gently. Sprinkle with the Parmesan cheese.

Serves 10

Firecracker Green Beans

2 pounds fresh green beans,
  trimmed and halved
1/4 cup vegetable oil
2 tablespoons whole black mustard seeds
4 garlic cloves, minced or pressed

1/2 teaspoon crushed red pepper flakes
2 teaspoons salt
1/2 teaspoon sugar
Freshly ground black pepper to taste

Cook the green beans in boiling water in a large stockpot for 3 to 4 minutes or until just tender. Drain immediately in a colander and rinse under cold running water to stop the cooking process; drain thoroughly. (You may blanch the green beans up to 1 day ahead and store, tightly covered, in the refrigerator.)

Heat the oil in a large deep stockpot over medium-high heat until hot but not smoking. Add the black mustard seeds and loosely cover. Cook for 20 seconds or until the mustard seeds pop to resemble popcorn. Add the garlic and red pepper flakes and sauté until the garlic begins to brown. Add the green beans, salt and sugar and stir to mix. Reduce the heat to medium-low and cook the beans for 7 to 8 minutes, stirring constantly. Season with pepper and serve.

Serves 8

Green Beans Provençale ♡

1 onion, coarsely chopped
4 garlic cloves, minced
2 tablespoons olive oil
4 large tomatoes, peeled and
  chopped
1/2 cup dry white wine
1 (2-ounce) can sliced black
  olives, drained

1 pound fresh green beans,
  trimmed
1/4 teaspoon lemon pepper
Salt and black pepper to taste
1 tablespoon lemon juice

Sauté the onion and garlic in the olive oil in a skillet for 5 minutes. Stir
in the tomatoes and wine and bring to a boil. Reduce the heat and simmer
for 20 minutes or until the liquid is mostly reduced, stirring occasionally.
Stir in the olives. Cook the green beans in boiling water in a saucepan for
10 minutes or until tender. Drain and keep warm until ready to serve.

To serve, place the green beans on a serving platter and sprinkle with the
lemon pepper, salt and black pepper. Spoon the sauce over the green beans
and drizzle with the lemon juice.

Serves 6

Green Beans with Roasted Onion Vinaigrette ♡

2 red onions (about 1 pound)
1 teaspoon olive oil
1/4 teaspoon fine grain sea salt, or
  to taste
1/4 teaspoon pepper, or to taste
2 sprigs of fresh thyme
1 tablespoon olive oil

1/2 tablespoon chopped fresh dill
3 tablespoons Champagne vinegar
1 tablespoon stone ground
  Dijon mustard
2 pounds green beans, trimmed,
  steamed and chilled

Preheat the oven to 400 degrees. Cut the onions into halves vertically and
drizzle the cut side of each with 1/4 teaspoon olive oil. Sprinkle the onion
halves evenly with the sea salt and pepper. Place 1 sprig of thyme on
1 onion half and top with another onion half to form a whole onion. Wrap
in foil to enclose. Repeat the procedure with the remaining onion halves and
sprigs of thyme.

Bake for 1 hour or until the onions are tender. Remove from the oven
and cool to room temperature. Unwrap the onions and discard the thyme.
Chop the onions and place in a bowl. Add 1 tablespoon olive oil, the dill,
Champagne vinegar and Dijon mustard and mix well. Add the green beans
and toss to coat.

Serves 8

Seasoning Etiquette

Salting your food before you taste it is a sacrilege in most chef's opinions, so don't do it! If someone asks you to pass the salt, always pass the salt and pepper together and place them on the table within the person's reach. Do not hand them to the person. This is also true for the cream and sugar.

Balsamic-Glazed Baby Carrots

^{1}/2 cup (1 stick) butter
3^{1}/2 pounds peeled baby carrots
6 tablespoons sugar
1 teaspoon minced fresh ginger
^{1}/3 cup balsamic vinegar
Salt and pepper to taste
^{1}/4 cup chopped fresh chives

Melt the butter in a wide heavy sauté pan over medium heat. Add the carrots and sauté for 5 minutes. Cover and cook for 7 minutes or until tender-crisp, stirring occasionally. Stir in the sugar, ginger and vinegar. Simmer, uncovered, for 10 to 12 minutes or until the carrots are tender and glazed, stirring frequently. (Do not allow the carrots to come to a rapid boil or the vinegar will burn.) Season with salt and pepper. Add the chives and toss to mix.

Serves 10 to 12

Cider-Glazed Carrots

9 cups julienned carrots
^{1}/4 cup packed brown sugar
2 tablespoons butter
2 tablespoons cider vinegar
^{1}/2 teaspoon dry mustard
^{1}/2 teaspoon paprika
^{1}/4 teaspoon salt
^{1}/8 teaspoon celery seeds
1^{1}/3 tablespoons chopped fresh parsley

Place the carrots in a large saucepan and cover with water. Bring to a boil and reduce the heat. Simmer for 1 minute or until tender; drain.

Combine the brown sugar, butter, cider vinegar, dry mustard, paprika, salt and celery seeds in a large nonstick skillet. Cook over low heat until the butter melts, stirring frequently. Bring to a boil and reduce the heat to medium. Add the carrots. Cook for 3 minutes or until the carrots are glazed and heated through, stirring constantly. Sprinkle with the parsley and toss to coat.

♡ Use 2 tablespoons canola oil instead of the butter for a heart-healthy alternative.

Serves 8 to 10

MEXICAN GRILLED CORN

MEXICAN CORN SPREAD
I cup mayonnaise
$1/4$ teaspoon cumin
I tablespoon chili powder
$1/4$ teaspoon kosher salt
$1/4$ cup chopped fresh cilantro
Juice of $1/2$ lime

CORN
8 to 10 ears of corn
Vegetable oil for brushing, or nonstick cooking spray
8 ounces Mexican Queso Añejo (Mexican aged cheese), finely crumbled

For the corn spread, combine the mayonnaise, cumin, chili powder, kosher salt, cilantro and lime juice in a bowl and mix well. (You may make ahead and chill in the refrigerator until ready to serve.)

For the corn, remove the husk and silk from the corn, leaving the stem intact to use as a handle. Brush each ear lightly with oil and place in a plastic bag. Chill in the refrigerator until ready to grill.

To serve, preheat the grill. Place the corn on a grill rack and grill over medium-high heat until lightly charred on all sides, turning occasionally. Brush the corn with the spread while still hot and roll in the cheese to coat.

Note: The Mexican Corn Spread can also be used as a condiment for hamburgers and other sandwiches to add a south-of-the-border flare.

Serves 8 to 10

Seared Corn Salsa with Smokey Chile Rub ♡ ⛩

Smokey Chile Rub

2 chipotle meco chiles
2 ancho chiles
2 tablespoons corn oil

2 1/2 teaspoons Mexican oregano
5 garlic cloves
1/2 cup kosher salt

Salsa

4 cups fresh corn (about 5 ears)
2 or 3 small jalapeño chiles or Serrano
   chiles, stemmed and chopped
   (including seeds)
2 tablespoons canola oil

1/2 cup chopped white onion
2 plum tomatoes, chopped
1 tablespoon fresh lime juice
1/4 cup chopped fresh cilantro

For the rub, remove the stems from the chiles and slit open with a knife. Remove the seeds and veins and open the chiles flat. Heat the corn oil in a heavy 8-inch skillet over medium heat until hot. Add the chiles and fry for 10 to 15 seconds or until puffed and darkened. Drain the chiles on paper towels and let stand until cool. Clean and dry the skillet.

Break the chiles into small pieces and process in a spice mill to form a fine powder. Heat the skillet over medium heat. Add the oregano and cook for 1 to 2 minutes until toasted, shaking the skillet to keep the oregano moving. (The oregano should darken a shade or two and smell fragrant.) Remove the oregano to a bowl to cool. Process the ground chiles, toasted oregano, garlic and kosher salt in a food processor until a fine but clumpy mixture forms.

Preheat the oven to the lowest setting. Spread the mixture in a thin even layer on a 10×15-inch baking sheet. Bake for 1 hour or until the mixture is dry and the clumps break apart when squeezed. Remove from the oven and cool thoroughly. Process in a food processor and store in an airtight container at room temperature. (This rub is delicious on beef and chicken and is even great sprinkled on eggs and popcorn.)

For the salsa, heat a large dry well-seasoned cast-iron skillet or nonstick skillet over medium-high heat. Add the corn and jalapeño chiles and cook until the kernels are light brown, stirring occasionally. Spoon into a bowl. Spoon the oil into the skillet and heat over medium-high heat. Add the onion and 1 1/2 teaspoons of the Smokey Chile Rub and cook until the onion is brown and crunchy. Add the corn mixture, tomatoes and lime juice and cook until hot, stirring constantly. Remove from the heat and cover. Let stand for 3 to 4 minutes. Stir in the cilantro and serve.

Serves 6 to 8

GRINDING SPICES

A coffee grinder dedicated to grinding spices is a useful tool in the well-equipped kitchen. Clean the grinder between uses by tearing stale bread into crumb-size pieces and processing in the grinder. Empty and wipe clean with a clean paper towel.

Fresh Fennel with Lemon & Parmesan

3 large fresh fennel bulbs
4 1/2 tablespoons extra-virgin olive oil
4 1/2 tablespoons fresh lemon juice
Salt and pepper to taste
1/4 cup (I ounce) grated Parmesan cheese

Trim the fennel bulbs and cut into quarters. Cut the quarters into very thin slices to measure about 9 cups and place in a large bowl. Drizzle with the olive oil and lemon juice and toss to coat. Season generously with salt and pepper and stir in the cheese. Let stand at room temperature for I hour or chill for up to 3 hours, tossing occasionally.

Note: This is a delicious side dish served with veal.

Serves 6

Braised Leeks

Great served on top of the Glazed Teriyaki Salmon on page 167.

2 leeks
I tablespoon olive oil
1/2 cup (about) low-salt chicken stock
1/4 cup (about) white wine

Remove the top 2/3 of the green part and the root end from the leeks. Clean the leeks and cut into julienne strips. Sauté in the olive oil in a skillet until a little color is showing. Add enough of the chicken stock and wine to cover the leeks halfway. Cover and simmer for 20 minutes, checking periodically to make sure that all of the liquid has not evaporated.

Serves 4

Smart Heart Freezer & Refrigerator Basics

Fill your freezer and refrigerator with heart smart vegetables such as spinach, carrots, dark leafy lettuce, and tomatoes for quick salads; a variety of frozen vegetables for when you run out of fresh; egg whites and whole eggs; fat-free yogurt and milk; flavorful cheeses that you can use sparingly such as feta cheese, blue cheese, and Parmesan cheese; salad dressing made from olive or canola oil; and even water-packed tofu.

Mushroom Casserole

2 pounds mixed variety of sliced mushrooms
4 chicken bouillon cubes
1/4 cup boiling water
2 tablespoons all-purpose flour
2 tablespoons grated Parmesan cheese
1 cup heavy cream
1 (8-ounce) package herb stuffing mix
1/2 cup (1 stick) salted butter, melted

Preheat the oven to 350 degrees. Place the mushrooms in a greased 9×13-inch baking dish. Dissolve the bouillon cubes in the boiling water in a saucepan. Add the flour, Parmesan cheese and cream. Cook until thickened, stirring constantly. (If the sauce becomes too thick, you may stir in 2 tablespoons milk.) Pour the sauce over the mushrooms.

Toss the stuffing mix and melted butter in a bowl and spoon evenly over the mushrooms. Cover with foil and bake for 40 minutes. Remove the foil and bake for 10 minutes longer.

Serves 8

Peas with Pancetta

1/4 cup olive oil
1 1/4 cups finely chopped onions
1/3 cup finely chopped pancetta or bacon (about 3 ounces)
4 (10-ounce) packages frozen petite peas, thawed
1/3 cup finely chopped fresh Italian parsley
1/3 cup canned reduced-sodium chicken broth
Salt and pepper to taste

Heat the olive oil in a large heavy skillet over medium-low heat. Add the onion and pancetta and sauté for 8 minutes or until the onion is tender. Add the peas, parsley and chicken broth and cook for 5 minutes or until the peas are heated through. Season with salt and pepper.

Serves 12

Sesame-Coated Sugar Snap Peas ♡

1 pound sugar snap peas, trimmed
2 teaspoons Oriental sesame oil
1 teaspoon olive oil
$^1/_4$ teaspoon ground ginger
2 teaspoons black sesame seeds
Salt and pepper to taste

Steam the peas for 3 minutes or until tender-crisp. Combine the sesame oil, olive oil and ginger in a small bowl and blend well. Add the peas and toss to coat. Add the sesame seeds and toss to coat. Season with salt and pepper.

Serves 6

Baby Red Potatoes with Goat Cheese, Pine Nuts & Mint

2 pounds baby red potatoes, cut into quarters
2 teaspoons kosher salt
$^1/_3$ cup olive oil
Kosher salt to taste
$^1/_4$ teaspoon pepper, or to taste
$^1/_2$ cup toasted pine nuts
$^1/_4$ cup sliced red onion
3 tablespoons julienned mint leaves
3 ounces goat cheese, crumbled into small pieces

Place the potatoes in a saucepan and add enough water to cover by 2 inches. Sprinkle with 2 teaspoons kosher salt. Bring to a boil and reduce the heat. Simmer, covered, for 15 minutes or until tender. Drain the potatoes and place in a bowl. Drizzle with the olive oil and season with kosher salt to taste and the pepper. Let stand until cool. Add the pine nuts, red onion, mint and goat cheese and toss gently until well incorporated. Serve at room temperature.

Serves 8

BAY LEAF RED-SKINNED ROASTED POTATOES

8 red-skinned potatoes
1/2 cup olive oil
40 small bay leaves
1 tablespoon coarse sea salt
2 teaspoons herbes de Provence
1 1/2 teaspoons coarsely cracked black pepper

Preheat the oven to 350 degrees. Cut 5 evenly spaced slices crosswise to, but not through, each potato and place in a 9×13-inch baking dish. Drizzle some of the olive oil over the potatoes and toss to coat. Slide 1 bay leaf into each cut in each potato. Mix the sea salt, herbes de Provence and pepper in a small bowl and sprinkle over the potatoes. Bake for 55 minutes or until roasted and tender. Drizzle with the remaining olive oil. Preheat the broiler. Broil for 4 minutes or until the potatoes begin to brown. Discard the bay leaves before serving.

Note: Herbes de Provence is a combination of dried herbs such as basil, marjoram, rosemary, sage, lavender, thyme, fennel seeds and summer savory.

Serves 4

CRUSHED POTATOES

2 large russet baking potatoes
Salt to taste
6 scallions
3/4 cup olive oil
Pepper to taste
1 cup fresh flat-leaf parsley, finely chopped

Peel the potatoes and cut into quarters. Place in a saucepan and add enough cold water to cover by 1 inch. Season with salt. Bring to a boil and reduce the heat. Simmer for 15 minutes or until tender. Drain the potatoes in a colander and let stand for 5 minutes.

Finely chop the white and light green parts of the scallions. Heat the olive oil and scallions in a saucepan over medium heat until the olive oil begins to sizzle. Add the potatoes and mash coarsely with a fork. (Do not mash completely.) Generously season the potatoes with salt and pepper and stir in the parsley.

Serves 6

CRISPY POTATO & SCALLION PANCAKES

2 large baking potatoes
5 scallions, thinly sliced with some green stems
Kosher salt to taste
$1/4$ cup canola oil
Pepper to taste

Peel the potatoes and coarsely grate into a large bowl. Add the scallions and kosher salt and mix well. Heat the oil in a large skillet over medium-high heat. Drop the potato mixture by 2 to 4 tablespoonfuls into the hot oil and press down with a spatula to form pancakes. Cook for 4 minutes on each side or until well-browned, turning once. Season with kosher salt and pepper while hot. Remove to paper towels to drain. (You may make the pancakes early in the day.)

Makes 6 pancakes

ROQUEFORT POTATO GRATIN

$5^1/2$ pounds russet potatoes
Salt and pepper to taste
2 cups heavy cream
5 ounces Roquefort cheese, crumbled
$1/2$ cup dry bread crumbs
$1^1/4$ teaspoon crumbled dried rosemary
$1/4$ cup ($1/2$ stick) butter, cut into small pieces

Preheat the oven to 425 degrees. Peel the potatoes and cut into slices $1/8$ inch thick. Layer the potatoes in a buttered 10×15-inch glass baking dish, sprinkling each layer with salt and pepper. Bring the cream to a boil in a heavy medium saucepan and reduce the heat to medium. Add the cheese and cook until melted, whisking constantly. Pour over the potatoes and cover with foil. Bake for 1 hour or until tender.

Preheat the broiler. Mix the bread crumbs and rosemary in a small bowl. Sprinkle over the potatoes and dot with the butter. Broil for 4 minutes or until the butter melts and the crumb mixture is golden brown, watching closely to prevent overbrowning. Remove from the oven and let stand for 10 minutes. Serve warm.

Note: You may use 3 ounces crumbled Gorgonzola cheese instead of Roquefort cheese for a more robust flavor.

Serves 8

*Place the potatoes in a saucepan
and add enough cold water to
cover by 1 inch. Having too
little water or too much water
spoils many boiled potatoes.
Cover the potatoes and
bring to a boil. Boil for 15 to
20 minutes or until the
potatoes begin to crack and are
fork tender. Drain the potatoes
and let stand for 3 minutes
before serving.*

BASIC GARLIC MASHED POTATOES

5 pounds Yukon gold potatoes, peeled and quartered
1 large yellow onion, thinly sliced
10 garlic cloves
2 teaspoons salt
$1/2$ cup (1 stick) unsalted butter, softened
2 cups light cream
Salt to taste
Freshly ground white pepper to taste
1 to 2 tablespoons butter, softened (optional)
$1/4$ cup light cream (optional)

Place the potatoes, onion, garlic and salt in a large stockpot and add cold water to cover. Bring to a boil and cook for 15 to 20 minutes or until the potatoes are tender. Drain the potato mixture in a colander. Place $1/2$ cup butter in the drained stockpot. Push the potato mixture through a ricer into the stockpot. Add 2 cups cream and beat well. Season with salt and white pepper and mix well. To keep the potatoes warm, make a well in the center of the potatoes and add 1 to 2 tablespoons butter and $1/4$ cup cream. Cover and place over very low heat until ready to serve. Beat until smooth when ready to serve.

Note: You can mash the potatoes with a masher, a fork or a mixer at low speed instead of using a ricer.

Variations:
For Cheddar Cheese Potatoes, add 1 cup (4 ounces) shredded sharp Cheddar cheese to the potato mixture.

For Bacon Cheddar Cheese Potatoes, add 1 cup crumbled cooked bacon and 1 cup (4 ounces) shredded sharp Cheddar Cheese to the potato mixture.

For Herb Potatoes, add 1 tablespoon chopped fresh rosemary, 1 tablespoon chopped fresh thyme, 1 tablespoon chopped fresh parsley and 1 tablespoon chopped fresh chives to the potato mixture just before serving.

For Blue Cheese Mushroom Potatoes, add 1 cup sautéed chopped mushrooms and $1/2$ cup crumbled blue cheese to the potato mixture.

For Sour Cream Chive Potatoes, reduce the light cream by 1 cup in the potato mixture and add 1 cup sour cream and 3 tablespoons chopped fresh chives, or to taste.

For Wasabi Potatoes, add wasabi paste to taste to the potato mixture.

Serves 10 to 12

Sweet Potato & Apple Gratin

3 tablespoons unsalted butter
1 pound Granny Smith apples or other
   tart apples, peeled, quartered and sliced
1 1/2 pounds sweet potatoes or yams,
   peeled and cut into thin rounds
2 tablespoons brown sugar
1 teaspoon ground cinnamon
1/4 teaspoon ground nutmeg
1 teaspoon salt
1/4 teaspoon ground white pepper
1 1/4 cups heavy cream
1/2 cup fresh bread crumbs
2 tablespoons unsalted butter

Preheat the oven to 375 degrees. Melt 3 tablespoons butter in a large skillet over medium-high heat. Add the apples and cook for 6 to 8 minutes or until the apples begin to caramelize.

Combine the sweet potatoes, brown sugar, cinnamon, nutmeg, salt and white pepper in a medium bowl and mix well. Pour in 1 cup of the cream and mix well. Layer 1/2 of the sweet potato mixture, slightly overlapping, in a buttered 9×9-inch baking dish. Cover with the apples and top with the remaining sweet potatoes. Pour the remaining 1/4 cup cream over the top. Cover with foil and bake for 1 hour or until the sweet potatoes are tender. Remove from the oven and increase the oven temperature to 500 degrees. Sprinkle the bread crumbs over the sweet potatoes and dot with 2 tablespoons butter. Bake until brown, watching carefully to prevent overbrowning. Remove and let stand for 10 minutes before serving.

Serves 6 to 8

Oven-Roasted Stuffed Acorn Squash

8 (4-inch-wide) acorn squash
1/4 cup (1/2 stick) unsalted butter, melted
5 shallots
2 (2 1/2-pound) butternut squash, cut into
   halves lengthwise and seeds removed
Salt and freshly ground pepper to taste
3 tablespoons heavy cream
1 1/4 teaspoons finely chopped fresh
   thyme

GARNISH
Sprigs of fresh thyme

Preheat the oven to 425 degrees. Remove the tops and seeds from the acorn squash. Cut a thin slice from the base of each and set upright on a baking sheet. Brush the tops with 1 tablespoon of the butter. Wrap the shallots loosely in foil. Bake the acorn squash and shallots for 40 minutes or until the shallots are soft and the acorn squash is golden. Remove from the oven and keep the squash warm. Let the shallots cool slightly.

Cut the butternut squash into halves lengthwise and remove the seeds. Brush the cut sides of the butternut squash with 1 tablespoon of the remaining butter and season with salt and pepper. Place cut side down on a baking sheet. Bake for 50 minutes or until tender. Remove from the oven to cool slightly.

Squeeze the shallots from their skins and coarsely chop. Scoop the pulp from the butternut squash into a bowl, discarding the skins. Add the shallots, 2 tablespoons remaining butter, the cream, thyme, salt and pepper and mash well. Spoon into the acorn squash and garnish each with a sprig of thyme.

Serves 8

Twice-Baked Butternut Squash with Apples & Maple Syrup ♡ ⑯

I large butternut squash
I yellow onion, coarsely chopped
I large Granny Smith apple, peeled and
   cut into wedges
I large garlic clove, minced

I tablespoon olive oil
Pinch of freshly ground nutmeg
Salt and pepper to taste
I egg
2 tablespoons pure maple syrup

Preheat the oven to 350 degrees. Cut the butternut squash into halves lengthwise. Peel each half and remove the seeds. Cut crosswise into slices 1/2 inch thick. Arrange the onion, apple and garlic in a 9×13-inch baking dish. Drizzle with the olive oil and season with the nutmeg, salt and pepper. Arrange the squash over the top and cover tightly with foil. Bake for I hour or until the squash is very tender. Maintain the oven temperature.

Process the squash mixture and any accumulated pan juices in a blender or food processor until puréed. Season with salt and pepper. (You can make up to 4 hours ahead at this point and store, covered, in the refrigerator.)

Stir the egg into the puréed squash mixture and return to the baking dish. Drizzle with the maple syrup. Bake for 25 minutes or until the juices along the edges bubble slightly.

Serves 6

Baked Herb-Stuffed Tomatoes ⑯

2 tomatoes, cut into halves horizontally
   and seeded
Salt to taste
1/3 cup fine fresh bread crumbs
1/4 cup (I ounce) grated Parmigiano-
   Reggiano cheese

1/4 cup minced shallots
1/2 teaspoon minced garlic
1/2 cup finely chopped fresh basil leaves
1/4 teaspoon dried thyme, crumbled
Pepper to taste
2 tablespoons extra-virgin olive oil

Sprinkle the inside of the tomatoes with salt and arrange cut side down on paper towels. Let stand for I hour to drain.

Preheat the oven to 400 degrees. Combine the bread crumbs, cheese, shallots, garlic, basil, thyme, salt and pepper in a bowl and stir to mix. Drizzle in the olive oil a small amount at a time, stirring after each addition. Arrange the tomato halves cut side up in a shallow baking pan and stuff with the bread crumb mixture. (You may make 4 hours in advance up to this point and keep at room temperature.)

Place the baking pan on a rack in the upper third of the oven and bake for 20 minutes or until the topping is golden brown. Do not overcook or the tomatoes will lose their shape. Remove from the oven and serve immediately.

Serves 4

Baked Cherry Tomatoes

2 tablespoons extra-virgin olive oil
2 (12-ounce) baskets cherry tomatoes
1 teaspoon salt
1 teaspoon pepper
1/4 cup chopped fresh Italian parsley
1/4 cup freshly grated Parmesan cheese

Preheat the oven to 400 degrees. Pour the oil into a 9×13-inch ceramic baking dish. Add the tomatoes and turn to coat well. Season with the salt and pepper. Sprinkle with the parsley and Parmesan cheese.

Bake for 10 minutes or until the tomatoes are plump and shiny. Serve hot or warm.

Serves 8

Gratin-Style Roasted Tomatoes

2 large tomatoes, sliced 1/2 inch thick
Salt and pepper to taste
2 tablespoons finely chopped fresh basil
1 tablespoon finely chopped fresh Italian parsley
2 tablespoons extra-virgin olive oil
1 garlic clove, minced
1 1/4 cups coarse fresh bread crumbs
1/3 cup freshly grated Parmesan cheese
1/2 teaspoon salt
1/2 teaspoon pepper

Preheat the oven to 500 degrees. Arrange the tomatoes, slightly overlapping, in an oiled pie pan. (Do not use a glass pie plate.) Season the tomatoes with salt and pepper to taste. Sprinkle with the basil and parsley.

Heat the olive oil in a small skillet over medium heat. Add the garlic and sauté for 1 minute. Remove from the heat. Mix the bread crumbs, Parmesan cheese, sautéed garlic, 1/2 teaspoon salt and 1/2 teaspoon pepper in a bowl. Sprinkle over the tomatoes. Bake for 15 minutes or until the crumbs are golden.

Serves 3 to 4

Tomato, Onion & Niçoise Olive Tart

Pastry Dough
2 cups all-purpose flour
3/4 cup (1 1/2 sticks) unsalted butter, cut into pieces
1 1/2 teaspoons salt
6 tablespoons very cold water

Tart
1 large sweet onion
1 large Spanish onion
2 tablespoons olive oil
8 ounces Gruyère cheese or Jack cheese, shredded
8 ounces plum tomatoes, cut into 1/2-inch wedges
8 ounces yellow tomatoes or plum tomatoes, cut into 1/2-inch wedges
1/4 cup pitted niçoise olives
Salt and pepper to taste

For the pastry dough, process the flour, butter and salt in a food processor to form pea-size crumbs. Add the cold water 1 tablespoon at a time, processing constantly until the mixture forms a ball. Knead on a floured surface 3 or 4 times. Shape into a ball and flatten. Wrap in plastic wrap and chill for 1 hour. (You may make 1 week ahead.)

For the tart, place the onions and olive oil in a heavy large skillet. Cover and cook over medium-low heat for 20 minutes or until softened, stirring occasionally. (The onions should taste sweet and mellow at this point.) Uncover and continue to cook until the liquid has evaporated and the onions are just golden, stirring occasionally. Do not brown. Remove from the heat to cool slightly.

Preheat the oven to 375 degrees. Roll the pastry into a 14-inch circle on a lightly floured surface. Fit into a 12-inch tart pan with a removable rim. Fold any excess dough over and press toward the center and side of the pan. Spread the onion mixture over the dough and top with the cheese. Arrange the tomatoes and olives in a circular pattern over the cheese. Season with salt and pepper.

Bake for 50 to 60 minutes or until the pastry is brown. Remove from the oven to cool slightly. Serve warm or at room temperature.

Note: You may use store-bought pastry dough instead of making your own.

Serves 6 to 8

PROSCIUTTO-WRAPPED ZUCCHINI

3 (4-ounce) zucchini
2 tablespoons olive oil
1/8 teaspoon salt
1/8 teaspoon freshly ground pepper

4 ounces imported prosciutto,
  thinly sliced
1/3 cup grated Parmesan cheese

Preheat the oven to 400 degrees. Cut the zucchini lengthwise into 4 wedges each. Combine the zucchini wedges, olive oil, salt and pepper in a bowl and toss to coat. Cut the proscoiutto into halves. Wrap each zucchini wedge with 1/2 slice of prosciutto. Place on a baking sheet and bake for 12 minutes. Remove from the oven and sprinkle each wedge with Parmesan cheese. Bake for 10 minutes longer. Serve immediately.

Serves 4 to 6

ROASTED VEGETABLE TIMBALES

1/2 cup olive oil
1 pound asparagus, trimmed
1 pound zucchini, cut into slices
  1/3 inch thick
1 pound yellow squash, cut into slices
  1/3 inch thick
2 red bell peppers, seeded and cut into
  bite-size squares
2 red onions, cut into slices 1/3 inch thick

1 pound red potatoes, cut into slices
  1/3 inch thick
Salt and pepper to taste
3/4 cup (3 ounces) ricotta cheese
1 teaspoon chopped fresh thyme
8 ounces mozzarella cheese, cut into
  6 (1/4-inch-thick) slices
6 sprigs of fresh rosemary

Preheat the oven to 400 degrees. Brush 2 baking sheets with some of the olive oil. Arrange the asparagus, zucchini, yellow squash, bell peppers, onions and potatoes in a single layer on the baking sheets and brush with a light coating of the remaining olive oil. Season with salt and pepper. Place on the lower or middle oven rack and bake for 10 to 15 minutes or until the vegetables are tender and light brown. Turn the vegetables and continue baking for 6 to 7 minutes or until tender and light brown. Remove from the oven and maintain the oven temperature.

Combine the ricotta cheese and chopped thyme in a bowl and mix well.

To assemble a timbale, arrange 2 slices of zucchini overlapping on a lightly oiled baking sheet. Stack 2 pieces of squash over the zucchini and spread 1 tablespoon of the ricotta cheese mixture over the squash. Continue layering and stacking with 2 potato slices, 1 onion slice, 1 mozzarella cheese slice and 2 or 3 red pepper slices. Spread 1 tablespoon of the remaining ricotta cheese mixture over the top of the stack and top with asparagus spears. Repeat the stacking process to form 5 more timbales. Trim the rosemary sprigs to be 1 inch taller than each timbale and remove the bottom leaves. Make a hole through each timbale with a metal skewer and insert 1 sprig of rosemary in each. Bake for 5 minutes or until the cheese melts and the vegetables are heated through. Serve warm or at room temperature.

Note: For an elegant presentation, assemble the timbales in individual cylinder molds lightly sprayed with cooking spray and gently remove before serving. You may also use other vegetables, such as eggplant, yellow bell peppers and Vidalia onions, when assembling the timbales and top with a slice of tomato instead of asparagus spears. Olive oil cooking spray may also be used to reduce the calories and fat.

Serves 6

GOLDEN COUSCOUS

1 cup chicken stock
1 cup fresh shelled or frozen peas
2 tablespoons butter
1/4 cup shallots, minced
1/4 cup dry white wine
2 tablespoons butter

1/4 teaspoon saffron powder, or
  1/2 teaspoon saffron threads, crumbled
1 1/4 cups couscous
1/4 cup chopped fresh chives
Salt and pepper to taste

Bring the chicken stock to a simmer in a small saucepan. Add the peas and cook for 1 to 2 minutes or until tender. Remove the peas to a bowl using a slotted spoon and keep warm. Reserve the chicken stock in the saucepan.

Melt 2 tablespoons butter in a medium saucepan with a tight-fitting lid. Add the shallots and sauté until translucent. Add the wine and cook until all of the liquid has evaporated.

Return the chicken stock to a gentle boil. Add 2 tablespoons butter and the saffron and continue to simmer. Stir into the sautéed shallots. Add the couscous and mix well. Cover tightly and remove from the heat. (Cover tightly with foil if the lid on your saucepan doesn't seal well.) Let stand for 5 to 8 minutes. Uncover and fluff the couscous with a fork. Gently stir in the peas and chives. Season with salt and pepper.

Serves 4

ORZO WITH CARAMELIZED ONIONS

This flavorful orzo will be sure to please your guests. Try serving it with the Raspberry-Marinated Beef Tenderloin or the Beef Tenderloin Steaks with Balsamic Sauce (both on page 144).

1/4 cup (1/2 stick) butter
2 onions, chopped
1 pound orzo

4 cups chicken broth, plus extra as needed
Salt and pepper to taste

Melt the butter in a skillet. Add the onions and sauté over low to medium heat for 20 minutes or until the onions are translucent and very soft.

Cook the orzo in the chicken stock in a saucepan using the package directions. Drain and add to the sautéed onions. Season with salt and pepper.

Note: You may add additional butter if you prefer a moister orzo.

Serves 8

BROILED POLENTA

Begin this dish early in the day to allow the polenta to set.

I to 2 tablespoons olive oil
6^1/$_2$ cups water
1^1/$_2$ teaspoons salt
2 cups polenta or yellow cornmeal (not stone-ground)
^{1}/$_2$ cup (2 ounces) grated Parmesan cheese

Brush a 9×13-inch baking pan with water. Brush a baking sheet with 2 teaspoons of the olive oil. Combine the water, salt and polenta in a large heavy saucepan. Bring to a boil over medium heat, whisking constantly. Reduce the heat to low. Cook for 20 to 25 minutes or until the polenta is very thick and pulls from the side of the pan, stirring constantly with a long handled wooden spoon. Spread evenly in the prepared baking pan using a dampened heat-proof spatula. Place on a rack and let stand for 30 minutes or until set and lukewarm.

Invert the polenta onto the prepared baking sheet to unmold. Brush a piece of parchment paper with some of the remaining olive oil and place oiled side down onto the top surface of the polenta. Cover the entire sheet tightly with plastic wrap and chill for 6 hours or longer. Remove from the refrigerator and bring to room temperature.

Set the oven rack 5 inches from the broiler and preheat the broiler. Brush the polenta with the remaining olive oil to coat lightly and sprinkle with the Parmesan cheese. Broil for 4 to 7 minutes or until pale golden brown. Remove from the oven and cool for 5 minutes. Cut into the desired shapes and sizes.

Serves 6

Photograph for this recipe is on page 158.

Persian Rice

2 cups Middle Eastern or Indian
  basmati rice
10 cups water
1 1/2 tablespoons salt

1/4 cup (1/2 stick) unsalted butter
2 tablespoons chopped fresh dill
1/2 cup coarsely chopped shelled unsalted
  undyed pistachios

Rinse the rice in cold water several times until the water runs clear and drain in a sieve. Bring 10 cups water and salt to a boil in a large heavy stockpot. Add the rice and boil, uncovered, for 5 minutes. Drain the rice in a large sieve.

Melt the butter in a tall narrow heavy stockpot and remove from the heat. Spoon a thin layer of rice over the bottom and sprinkle lightly with the dill and pistachios. Continue layering and mounding in the order listed until all of the ingredients are used, ending with the rice. Make 5 or 6 holes in the rice to the bottom of the pot using the round long handle of a wooden spoon. Cover the stockpot with a kitchen towel and a heavy lid. Fold the edges of the towel up over the lid and secure with a string to prevent the towel from burning. Cook the rice over medium-low heat for 30 to 35 minutes or until the rice is tender and forms a crust on the bottom; do not stir.

Spoon the rice onto a platter and dip the bottom of the stockpot in a large bowl of cold water for 30 seconds to loosen the crust from the bottom of the pan (tah-dig). Remove the crust with a large spoon and serve in a separate bowl or over the loose rice.

Serves 6 to 8

Fragrant Yellow Rice

For a great tasting meal, serve this recipe along with Firecracker Green Beans on page 120 and your favorite chicken recipe.

3 cups long-grain rice or basmati rice
10 cups water
2 teaspoons salt
1 teaspoon turmeric
5 whole cloves

1 (1 1/2-inch) stick of cinnamon
4 bay leaves
1/4 cup (1/2 stick) unsalted butter, cut
  into small pieces

Rinse the rice in several changes of water and drain. Place the rice in a bowl and pour 6 cups of the water over the rice. Let soak for 30 minutes and drain.

Bring the drained rice, the remaining 4 cups of water, the salt, turmeric, cloves, cinnamon stick and bay leaves to a boil in a heavy 3-quart saucepan with a tight-fitting lid. Stir the rice and cover the saucepan with foil and the lid, making sure to tighten the foil around the saucepan. Reduce the heat to very low and cook for 25 minutes. Remove from the heat and let the saucepan stand covered and undisturbed for 10 minutes. Uncover and remove the cloves, cinnamon stick and bay leaves. Add the butter and mix gently with a fork.

Serves 8 to 10

Wild Rice Braised with Aromatic Vegetables

I cup wild rice, rinsed well
2 cups water
I tablespoon unsalted butter
3 tablespoons finely chopped celery
3 tablespoons finely chopped onion
3 tablespoons finely chopped carrot
1/4 cup dry white wine or dry white French vermouth
1 1/2 cups (more or less) low-sodium chicken broth or homemade broth
I teaspoon salt
I teaspoon freshly ground pepper
I tablespoon butter (optional)

Simmer the rice in the water in a saucepan for 15 minutes. Drain and rinse the rice in fresh water. Melt I tablespoon butter in a tall saucepan over medium-low heat. Add the celery, onion and carrot and sauté until the vegetables are tender but not brown. Add the rice and sauté for 2 to 3 minutes, being sure to coat the rice with the butter from the vegetables. Add the wine and cook until most of the liquid evaporates, stirring constantly. Add enough chicken broth to the rice mixture to cover by 1/4 inch and bring to a simmer. Stir in the salt and pepper. Cook over low heat for 15 minutes or to the desired consistency, adding additional broth if needed to complete the cooking process. Unover and gently boil off any excess liquid, stirring constantly. Stir in I tablespoon butter to give the rice extra richness.

♡ For a heart-healthy version, substitute I tablespoon canola oil for the butter used to sauté the aromatic vegetables, reduce the salt to 1/2 teaspoon, and omit the optional butter at the end of the recipe. This recipe should serve 6 for heart healthy servings.

Serves 4

Mirepoix: Diced Aromatic Vegetables

To prepare mirepoix, or diced aromatic vegetables, melt 3 tablespoons butter in a small heavy saucepan over low heat. Add 1/3 cup finely chopped carrots, 1/3 cup finely chopped celery and 1/3 cup finely chopped onion and sauté slowly for 5 minutes. Stir in a pinch of dried thyme and continue sautéing until the vegetables are tender but not brown. Season with salt and pepper to taste. Use for flavoring rice, sauces, meats, and vegetables. You can make a large batch and freeze in ice cube trays for later use. Each cube is approximately the equivalent of 1 1/2 tablespoons. This recipe makes 1/3 to 1/2 cup.

Pennsylvania Farmhouse Stuffing

1 1/2 pounds day-old challah
1 pound sweet Italian sausage, casings removed
1/2 cup (1 stick) butter
1 large onion, finely chopped
2 ribs celery, finely chopped
1 cup finely chopped fennel
2 Granny Smith apples, chopped
1/4 cup chopped fresh sage
2 tablespoons chopped fresh flat-leaf parsley
1 tablespoon chopped fresh thyme
Salt and pepper to taste
1 cup chicken stock
1 egg
1/2 cup heavy cream

Preheat the oven to 350 degrees. Cut the bread into 1/2-inch cubes. Brown the sausage in a skillet, stirring until crumbly; drain. Melt the butter in a large sauté pan over medium-low heat. Add the onion, celery and fennel and cook until translucent, stirring frequently. Remove from the heat and stir in the apples, sage, parsley, thyme, salt, pepper, sausage and bread cubes.

Whisk the chicken stock, egg and cream in a bowl. Add to the stuffing mixture gradually, stirring well after each addition until all of the cream mixture is incorporated. Spoon into a buttered 2-quart baking dish. Cover and bake for 20 minutes. Uncover and bake for 25 minutes longer or until brown.

Serves 6 to 8

RED & WHITE PICKLED ONIONS

I pound Vidalia onions
I pound red onions
6 (4-inch) sprigs of fresh rosemary
2 cups white wine vinegar
I 1/2 cups water
I cup sugar
I tablespoon (heaping) pickling spice
2 teaspoons coarse kosher salt
2 garlic cloves

Cut the Vidalia onions and red onions into thin slices and separate into rings. Layer the Vidalia onions, red onions and rosemary 1/3 at a time in a 2-quart jar with a tight-fitting lid. Bring the vinegar, water, sugar, pickling spice, kosher salt and garlic cloves to a boil in a medium saucepan over high heat. Boil until the sugar dissolves, stirring constantly. Reduce the heat and simmer for 2 minutes, stirring frequently. Pour over the onion layers, pushing the onions into the liquid. Add enough cold water to cover the onions if needed. Let stand until cool. Replace the lid on the jar and chill for at least 24 hours before serving. (You may make up to 2 weeks ahead and store in the refrigerator.)

Makes 2 quarts

CRANBERRY-ORANGE RELISH

I large navel orange, rinsed
I (12-ounce) package fresh cranberries
2/3 cup sugar, or more to taste
2 tablespoons minced crystallized ginger
1/4 teaspoon ground allspice

Remove the stem from the orange and cut out the navel with a knife. Cut the orange into halves across the sections and remove any seeds. Chop the halves into small pieces. Pulse in a food processor until coarsely chopped and place in a bowl.

Rinse and sort the cranberries; drain. Pulse the cranberries in a food processor until coarsely chopped and add to the oranges. Add the sugar, crystallized ginger and allspice and stir to blend well. Cover and chill for 8 to 12 hours to allow the flavors to develop. (You may make up to 5 days ahead and store, covered, in the refrigerator.)

Makes about 3 cups

MAIN DISHES

Raspberry-Marinated Beef Tenderloin

1 cup raspberry vinegar
2 tablespoons olive oil
1 onion, finely chopped
1 carrot, finely chopped

1 garlic clove, sliced
2 bay leaves
1 (8-pound) cracked beef tenderloin,
   trimmed to 6³/4 to 7 pounds

Bring the raspberry vinegar, olive oil, onion, carrot, garlic and bay leaves to a boil in a saucepan. Remove from the heat to cool. Place the beef in a baking dish and pour the cooled marinade over the top. Cover and marinate in the refrigerator for 8 to 12 hours.

Preheat the oven to 500 degrees. Drain the beef, discarding the marinade. Place the beef on a rack in a roasting pan and bake for 10 minutes. Reduce the heat to 350 degrees and bake for 40 minutes longer for medium-rare. Remove from the oven and let stand to cool. (The beef will continue to cook as it cools.) Serve at room temperature.

Serves 12 to 14

Beef Tenderloin Steaks with Balsamic Sauce

Balsamic Sauce
¹/4 cup dry red wine
¹/4 cup high-quality sherry
3 tablespoons balsamic vinegar
1 shallot, minced

2 garlic cloves, minced
1 teaspoon sugar
1 egg yolk
¹/3 cup unsalted butter, melted

Steak
4 (6-ounce) beef tenderloin steaks
1 tablespoon coarse grain sea salt

1 tablespoon freshly ground pepper
2 tablespoons olive oil

For the sauce, bring the wine, sherry, balsamic vinegar, shallot, garlic and sugar to a boil in a small saucepan. Cook for 2 to 3 minutes or until the sugar is dissolved, stirring occasionally. Remove from the heat to cool. Whisk the egg yolk into the wine mixture. Cook over low heat for 4 to 5 minutes or until thickened, whisking constantly. Whisk in the butter until blended.

For the steaks, preheat the oven to 350 degrees. Rub the steaks with sea salt and pepper. Heat the olive oil in an ovenproof skillet over high heat. Add the steaks and cook for 2 to 3 minutes on each side or until brown. Place in the oven and bake for 8 to 10 minutes or to desired degree of doneness.

To serve, place the steaks on individual serving plates and spoon the sauce over the top.

Serves 4

GRILLED SIRLOIN WITH SHALLOT SOY SAUCE

Courtesy of Jean-George Vongerichten

1 cup regular or low-sodium soy sauce
1/2 cup rice vinegar
3 garlic cloves, thinly sliced
2 shallots, thinly sliced
1 to 2 tablespoons honey
1/2 tablespoon black peppercorns
1/4 cup fresh lime juice
1/4 cup (1/2 stick) unsalted butter
1 tablespoon freshly ground pepper to taste
2 tablespoons unsalted butter
1 1/2 pounds mixed mushrooms, such as creminis, oysters and
    stemmed shiitakes, cut into 1/2-inch pieces
1 tablespoon minced fresh ginger
2 tablespoons finely chopped chives
Salt and freshly ground pepper to taste
4 (6-ounce) boneless sirloin steaks, 1/2 inch thick
2 tablespoons vegetable oil

Combine the soy sauce, rice vinegar, garlic, shallots, honey and black peppercorns in a small saucepan. Simmer over medium heat for 15 minutes or until the sauce is reduced by 1/3. Remove from the heat and cool to room temperature. Cover and chill for 8 to 12 hours.

Strain the sauce into a small saucepan and add the lime juice, 1/4 cup butter and 1 tablespoon pepper. Simmer over medium heat for 2 minutes. Remove from the heat and keep warm.

Melt 2 tablespoons butter in a large skillet over medium-high heat. Heat until the foam subsides and add the mushrooms and ginger. Cook for 10 minutes or until the mushrooms are brown and almost tender, stirring occasionally. Remove from the heat and stir in the chives. Season with salt and pepper to taste.

Season the steaks with salt and pepper to taste. Heat the oil in a large skillet over high heat. Add the steaks and cook for 2 minutes per side for medium-rare. (You may omit the oil and grill on a grill rack.) Spoon 2 tablespoons of the sauce onto each of 4 serving plates. Place the steaks on the sauce and cover with the mushroom mixture. Serve with the remaining sauce.

Serves 4

CHILIED FLANK STEAK

1 flank steak, about 1 1/2 pounds
1/3 cup regular or spicy vegetable juice cocktail or Bloody Mary mix
1/3 cup soy sauce
1/4 cup canola oil
1/3 cup firmly packed dark brown sugar
2 garlic cloves, minced
1 tablespoon chili powder
1/8 teaspoon cumin

Score the steak on both sides with a sharp knife, cutting about 1/8 inch deep and forming a diamond pattern. Whisk the vegetable juice cocktail, soy sauce, oil, brown sugar, garlic, chili powder and cumin in a bowl. Pour 1/2 of the marinade into a nonaluminum pan and place the steak in the mixture. Pour the remaining marinade over the steak. Cover and marinate in the refrigerator for 24 hours, turning the steak at least once.

Drain the steak 30 minutes prior to grilling, reserving the marinade. Place the steak on a grill rack and grill to the desired degree of doneness. Pour the reserved marinade into a small saucepan and bring to a boil. Boil for 1 minute and remove from the heat. Strain into a small bowl and keep warm.

To serve, cut the steak diagonally across the grain into slices about 1/4 inch thick. Arrange on a warm platter or on individual serving plates. Serve with the sauce.

Note: You may use top round, London broil or skirt steak instead of the flank steak.

Serves 4

CHIMICHURRI SAUCE

For Chimichurri Sauce, purée 1 cup fresh flat-leaf parsley, 5 garlic cloves, minced, 1 teaspoon salt, 1/2 teaspoon white pepper, 1/2 teaspoon minced jalapeño chile, 2 tablespoons chopped fresh oregano, 2 tablespoons minced shallot, 3 tablespoons lemon juice and 3 tablespoons sherry vinegar in a blender. Add 1 cup olive oil in a fine stream and blend until emulsified. Drizzle over your favorite grilled steak.

Mahogany Beef Stew with Red Wine & Hoisin Sauce

2 tablespoons olive oil
3¹/₂ pounds boneless beef chuck roast, cut into 2¹/₂-inch pieces
Fine sea salt and freshly ground pepper to taste
2 tablespoons olive oil
3¹/₂ cups chopped yellow onions
1 cup Cabernet Sauvignon
1 (14-ounce) can diced tomatoes with Italian herbs
¹/₂ cup hoisin sauce
2 bay leaves
1 pound carrots, peeled and cut diagonally into 1-inch slices
1 cup Cabernet Sauvignon
2 tablespoons all-purpose flour
1 tablespoon butter, softened
2 tablespoons chopped fresh parsley

Heat 2 tablespoons olive oil in a heavy stockpot over high heat. Season the beef with sea salt and pepper and add to the hot olive oil. Sauté for 10 minutes or until brown on all sides. Remove the beef to a warm platter with a slotted spoon.

Reduce the heat to medium and add 2 tablespoons olive oil to the stockpot. Add the onions and sauté for 15 minutes or until golden brown. Return the beef to the stockpot. Add 1 cup wine, undrained tomatoes, hoisin sauce and bay leaves and bring to a rolling boil. Reduce the heat to low. Cover and simmer for 45 minutes, stirring occasionally.

Add the carrots and 1 cup wine. Cover and simmer for 30 minutes. Uncover and increase the heat to high. Cook for 15 minutes or until slightly thickened, stirring occasionally. Do not boil. Reduce the heat to medium. Stir in a mixture of the flour and butter. Simmer for 8 minutes or until thickened. Discard the bay leaves. Adjust the seasonings to taste. Sprinkle with the parsley.

Serves 6

Hoisin Sauce

Hoisin sauce is a thick mixture of ground soybeans, garlic, chiles, and spices. It is used in Chinese cooking as an ingredient or condiment and can be found in Asian supermarkets or the Asian section in your local grocery.

Navajo Stew

1 1/2 pounds beef chuck, cut into 1-inch
  cubes
2 tablespoons all-purpose flour
2 tablespoons olive oil
1 cup chopped onion
1 red bell pepper, chopped
1 jalapeño chile, chopped
2 teaspoons chili powder

1 teaspoon cumin
1 teaspoon salt
1 teaspoon pepper
3 garlic cloves, minced
1 (14-ounce) can diced tomatoes, or
  4 tomatoes, seeded and chopped
1 1/2 cups fresh or frozen corn
Hot cooked Spanish yellow rice

Lightly coat the beef with the flour. Heat 1 tablespoon of the olive oil in a Dutch oven. Add the beef and sauté until brown, working in batches if needed. Remove the beef with a slotted spoon to a bowl and keep warm. Add the remaining 1 tablespoon olive oil to the Dutch oven. Add the onion, bell pepper, jalapeño chile, chili powder, cumin, salt and pepper and sauté for 10 minutes or until the vegetables are tender. Add the garlic and cook for 2 minutes. Add the beef and any accumulated juices, tomatoes and corn. Cover and simmer over low heat for 1 1/2 hours or until the beef is tender. Adjust the seasonings to taste. Serve over hot Spanish yellow rice.

Note: You may use pork or venison instead of the beef. For a thinner stew, you may add canned beef broth.

Serves 4 to 6

Shiitake Mushroom Meatballs

Not your mother's Swedish meatballs, this recipe is great to serve for dinner on a cold winter day—kids love it.

1 pound meatball or meat loaf mix with
  beef, veal and pork
3/4 cup dry bread crumbs
1/2 cup milk
1/2 teaspoon salt
1/4 teaspoon ground allspice
1/4 teaspoon ginger
1/4 teaspoon pepper
1 egg white

4 1/2 cups thinly sliced shiitake mushroom
  caps (about 8 ounces)
1 1/2 cups thinly sliced carrots
1/2 cup thinly sliced shallots
2 tablespoons all-purpose flour
1 (10-ounce) can beef consommé
1/2 cup water
1/2 cup sour cream
1/2 cup chopped fresh parsley
Hot cooked egg noodles

Mix the meatball mix, bread crumbs, milk, salt, allspice, ginger, pepper and egg white in a bowl. Shape into thirty 1-inch meatballs. Spray a large nonstick skillet with nonstick cooking spray and heat over medium heat. Add the meatballs and cook for 8 minutes or until brown. Remove the meatballs from the skillet and keep warm. Add the mushrooms, carrots and shallots to the skillet and sauté for 5 minutes. Stir in the flour and cook for 1 minute. Whisk in the consommé gradually. Bring to a boil and return the meatballs to the skillet. Cover and reduce the heat. Simmer for 8 minutes. Add the water and cook for 2 minutes. Remove from the heat and stir in the sour cream and parsley. Serve over hot egg noodles.

Make-Ahead Note: You may make the meatballs ahead and store in the freezer.

Serves 4 to 6

GRILLED VEAL CHOPS WITH ROASTED POBLANO CREAM SAUCE

ROASTED POBLANO CREAM SAUCE

4 medium-large poblano chiles
2 tablespoons canola oil
1 white onion, thickly sliced
2 large garlic cloves
1/4 teaspoon dried Mexican oregano

1/2 teaspoon dried thyme
1/2 cup heavy cream
1/2 cup crème fraîche
1/4 cup chopped fresh cilantro
1/2 teaspoon salt

VEAL AND SAUTÉED MUSHROOMS

4 veal rib chops, 1 inch thick
2 tablespoons olive oil
2 garlic cloves

2 teaspoons Smokey Chile Rub (page 124)
2 tablespoons unsalted butter
8 ounces sliced shiitake or oyster mushrooms

GARNISH
Chopped fresh cilantro

For the sauce, heat a gas stovetop to medium-high and lay the whole chiles directly on the burner grates. Roast for 4 to 6 minutes or until the skin blisters and turns black, turning frequently with tongs. (You may also broil as close to the heat source as possible for 8 to 10 minutes.) Place the chiles in a bowl and cover with a towel. Let stand for 10 minutes. Peel the chiles, removing the stems and seeds. Rinse quickly with a small amount of water to remove any remaining skin or seed bits. Do not saturate the chiles. Pat dry and cut into 1/4-inch strips.

Heat the canola oil in a large frying pan. Add the onion and cook for 6 minutes or until seared and brown but still crunchy. Press the garlic through a press into the pan and add the oregano and thyme. Cook for 1 minute, stirring constantly. Add the roasted chiles and cook until heated through, stirring constantly. Reserve 1/3 of the mixture. (This onion/chile mixture is called poblano *rajas*.) Add the heavy cream to the remaining rajas and simmer for 5 minutes. Scrape into a food processor and add the crème fraîche and process until smooth, stopping to scrape down the side. (The consistency should be of a thick cream soup. If it is too thick, thin with a small amount of water.) Place in a small saucepan and add the cilantro and salt. Chop the reserved rajas to a rough dice and add to the sauce. Gently heat until just below a simmer, being careful not to scorch. (The sauce may be made a day in advance and stored in the refrigerator until ready to heat for serving.)

For the veal and mushrooms, place the veal chops on a platter and drizzle with the olive oil, turning to evenly coat. Press the garlic and rub over the veal chops to evenly coat. Sprinkle both sides with the smokey chile rub. Let stand at room temperature for 1 hour, turning several times. Preheat the grill to a medium-hot temperature. Place the veal on a grill rack and grill over direct flame with the lid loosely covering for 5 minutes per side. Remove to indirect heat and continue to grill for 3 to 5 minutes or to the desired degree of doneness. Remove to a heated platter. Melt the butter in a small skillet over medium heat. Add the mushrooms and sauté until soft and brown and the juices are released. Keep on low heat to keep warm.

To serve, place each veal chop on a bed of the cream sauce on individual serving plates. Drizzle with some of the cream sauce and top with a spoonful of the mushrooms. Garnish with chopped cilantro. Serve the remaining cream sauce on the side.

♡ For a heart-healthy version, use 1 tablespoon olive oil on the chops, brown the onions in a nonstick skillet coated with nonstick cooking spray and serve the *rajas* over the chops without the cream or mushrooms.

Serves 4

Veal Chops St. Tropez

4 (10- to 12-ounce) veal chops,
  1 to 1^1/$_2$ inches thick
Salt and pepper to taste
1 tablespoon olive oil
^{1}/$_2$ tablespoon butter
1 tablespoon olive oil
^{1}/$_2$ large onion, thinly sliced
^{1}/$_4$ cup chopped celery
^{1}/$_4$ cup chopped fresh Italian parsley

1 garlic clove, chopped
1^1/$_2$ pounds ripe plum tomatoes, peeled
  and coarsely chopped
2 anchovies, mashed
^{1}/$_2$ cup white wine
1 cup fresh basil, torn into bite-size pieces

GARNISH
Sprigs of fresh basil

Preheat the oven to 400 degrees. Pat the veal dry and season with salt and pepper. Heat 1 tablespoon olive oil and ^{1}/$_2$ tablespoon butter in a heavy ovenproof 12-inch skillet over medium-high heat. Add the veal and sear for 3 minutes on each side. Bake the chops in the same skillet for 10 to 15 minutes or to the desired degree of doneness. Heat 1 tablespoon olive oil in a heavy skillet over medium heat. Add the onion, celery, parsley and garlic and sauté for 10 minutes or until the onion is tender. Add the tomatoes, anchovies and white wine. Cover and cook for 15 minutes, stirring occasionally. Stir in the torn basil and season with salt and pepper. Place the veal chops on a serving platter and spoon the warm sauce over the top. Garnish with sprigs of fresh basil.

Variation:
For Grilled Tuna St. Tropez, use four 6-ounce tuna steaks about 1 inch thick instead of the veal. Grill for 3 minutes on each side for medium-rare or to the desired degree of doneness. Serve with the sauce.

Serves 4

Roasted Rack of Lamb with Rosemary-Garlic Sauce

LAMB
1 rack of lamb
1 teaspoon minced garlic
^{1}/$_2$ teaspoon chopped fresh thyme

^{1}/$_2$ teaspoon chopped fresh rosemary
^{1}/$_2$ teaspoon salt
Pinch of pepper

ROSEMARY-GARLIC SAUCE
1 cup fresh rosemary
1 cup garlic cloves

4 cups lamb or chicken stock
4 cups brown sauce (lamb or veal)

For the lamb, preheat the oven to 425 degrees. Rub the lamb with the garlic, thyme, rosemary, salt and pepper. Place on a rack in a roasting pan and bake for 16 to 20 minutes for a large rack of lamb or 12 to 15 minutes for a small rack of lamb.

For the sauce, combine the rosemary, garlic and lamb stock in a saucepan and cook until the garlic is tender. Add the brown sauce and simmer for 10 to 15 minutes. Process in batches in a blender until puréed. Strain into a serving bowl, discarding the solids. To serve, slice the lamb and serve with the sauce.

Note: Brown sauce may be purchased at the farmers markets or your local specialty food store.

Serves 2

Asian Barbecued Rack of Lamb

2 (1 1/2-pound) racks of lamb
Salt and pepper to taste
2 tablespoons canola oil
2/3 cup hoisin sauce
1/2 cup sugar
1/2 cup honey

1/2 cup chili garlic sauce
1/4 cup rice vinegar
2 tablespoons minced garlic
2 tablespoons minced fresh ginger
2 tablespoons low-sodium soy sauce
2 tablespoons sesame oil

Preheat the oven to 350 degrees. Slice the racks of lamb into meaty double chops (2 bones per chop). Season with salt and pepper and sear the chops in the canola oil in a large sauté pan over medium-high heat for 1 to 2 minutes per side or until brown.

Combine the hoisin sauce, sugar, honey, chili garlic sauce, rice vinegar, garlic, ginger, soy sauce and sesame oil in a bowl and mix well. Dip the seared chops into the sauce mixture and arrange on a rack placed over a parchment-lined baking sheet. Bake for 15 to 18 minutes for medium-rare or 20 to 23 minutes for medium. Remove from the oven and vent with foil. Let stand for 5 minutes before serving.

Bring the remaining sauce mixture to a boil in a saucepan. Reduce the heat and simmer for 10 minutes. Serve the chops with the sauce on the side for dipping.

Note: The sauce is also great to use as a marinade for chicken wings.

Serves 4

Marinated Butterflied Leg of Lamb

1 (5- to 6-pound) leg of lamb, boned and
   butterflied to a fairly even thickness
1/4 cup minced onion
1 or 2 garlic cloves, minced
1 tablespoon chopped fresh rosemary
1 tablespoon chopped fresh thyme
1/2 teaspoon dried thyme

1 tablespoon chopped fresh flat-leaf
   parsley
1 teaspoon salt
1/2 teaspoon pepper
1/2 cup canola oil
1/2 cup lemon juice, or to taste

Place the lamb in a sealable plastic bag. Process the onion, garlic, rosemary, fresh thyme, dried thyme, parsley, salt, pepper, canola oil and lemon juice in a blender until blended. Pour over the lamb and seal the bag. Marinate in the refrigerator for 8 to 12 hours. Let stand at room temperature for 1 hour before grilling.

Preheat the grill. Drain the lamb, reserving the marinade. Place the lamb on a grill rack and grill for 20 to 25 minutes, basting frequently with the reserved marinade.

Serves 6

Java Pork Tenderloin with Mango Habanero Salsa

Pork

1/2 cup medium-ground good-quality
   mocha java coffee beans
1/2 cup blended oil
1/4 cup molasses
1/4 cup ground macadamia nuts
1/4 cup pure maple syrup
1 jalapeño chile

1/2 tablespoon fresh minced ginger
1/2 tablespoon fresh minced garlic
1/2 tablespoon kosher salt
1/2 tablespoon freshly ground pepper
1 tablespoon mirin (Japanese rice wine)
Juice of 1 lime
1 (2-pound) whole pork tenderloin

Mango Habanero Salsa

1 fresh mango, chopped
3 plum tomatoes, chopped
1 habanero chile, minced
1/2 red onion, chopped

2 tablespoons cilantro, cut into ribbons
Juice of 1 lime
Juice of 1 orange
Salt and pepper to taste

For the pork, process the coffee beans, oil, molasses, macadamia nuts, maple syrup, jalapeño chile, ginger, garlic, kosher salt, pepper, mirin and lemon juice in a food processor until smooth. Place the pork in a sealable plastic bag. Pour the marinade over the pork and seal the bag. Marinate in the refrigerator for 36 to 48 hours, turning several times.

Preheat the grill. Drain the pork, discarding the marinade. Place the pork on a grill rack and grill, covered, over a medium flame for 15 to 25 minutes or until a meat thermometer inserted into the thickest part of the meat registers 165 degrees. Remove from the grill and let stand at room temperature for 10 minutes before serving.

For the salsa, combine the mango, tomatoes, habanero chile, onion, cilantro, lime juice, orange juice, salt and pepper in a bowl and mix well.

To serve, carve the pork and serve with the salsa.

Serves 4 to 6

Seating

*Formal dinners are often occasions for guests of
honor and formal toasting! The most honored guest sits in the
seat to the right of the host. The second most honored seat is
to the right of the co-host.*

Jalapeño Grilled Pork

3 jalapeño chiles, seeded and chopped
2 garlic cloves
1 plum tomato, peeled, seeded and chopped
$1/4$ cup lime juice
2 tablespoons chopped fresh cilantro
$1/4$ teaspoon salt
1 (3-pound) boneless pork loin roast
$1/4$ cup ($1/2$ stick) butter
2 or 3 jalapeño chiles, seeded and chopped
1 teaspoon salt
Gourmet salad greens

Mix 3 jalapeño chiles, the garlic, tomato, lime juice, cilantro and $1/4$ teaspoon salt in a bowl. Butterfly the pork by cutting lengthwise down the center of the flat side to within $1/2$ inch of the bottom and then cutting $1/2$ inch horizontally from the bottom to the left and right. Open the pork and place between 2 sheets of heavy-duty plastic wrap. Pound with a meat mallet or rolling pin to flatten the pork to $1/2$ inch thick. Spread the jalapeño chile mixture over the pork. Roll up and tie with string at 1 inch intervals. Place seam side down in a lightly greased 7×11-inch baking dish. Cover and chill for 8 hours.

Preheat the grill. Mix the butter, 2 or 3 jalapeño chiles and 1 teaspoon salt in a bowl. Place the pork on a grill rack and grill, covered, over medium-high heat for 40 minutes or until a meat thermometer inserted into the thickest portion registers 160 degrees, turning and basting frequently with the butter mixture. Cut into slices and serve with gourmet greens.

Serves 8

Pork Medallions with Cider Sauce

Cider Sauce
$2^1/2$ tablespoons unsalted butter
4 garlic cloves, minced
1 tablespoon dry mustard
$1^1/2$ tablespoons all-purpose flour

3 cups chicken stock or broth
3 cups beef stock or broth
2 cups apple cider

Pork
$2^1/4$ pounds pork tenderloins, cut into
  1-inch-thick rounds
All-purpose flour

Salt and pepper to taste
2 tablespoons butter
$1/2$ cup Calvados or applejack

For the sauce, melt the butter in a large heavy saucepan over medium heat. Add the garlic and dry mustard and sauté for 30 seconds. Add the flour and cook for 2 minutes, stirring constantly. Whisk in the chicken stock, beef stock and cider gradually. Boil for 45 minutes or until reduced to a sauce consistency, stirring occasionally.

For the pork, pound the pork between 2 sheets of waxed paper until $1/2$ inch thick. Coat with a mixture of flour, salt and pepper. Melt the butter in a large skillet over high heat. Add the pork in batches and cook for 2 minutes per side or until cooked through. Return all of the pork to the skillet and remove from the heat. Add the Calvados and ignite with a match, being very careful. Let the flames subside and reheat. Boil until most of the liquid evaporates.

To serve, place the pork in a serving bowl and spoon the sauce over the top.

Serves 6

Grilled Teriyaki Pork Chops with Ginger Peach Salsa

1 cup chopped peaches
$1/2$ cup chopped plums
$1/4$ cup minced shallots
3 tablespoons orange juice
2 tablespoons chopped fresh parsley
1 teaspoon grated lime zest
2 tablespoons fresh lime juice
$1^1/2$ tablespoons chopped jalapeño chile
1 tablespoon minced fresh mint
1 tablespoon honey

1 teaspoon minced fresh ginger
4 (6-ounce) center-cut pork chops,
  about 1 inch thick
$1/4$ cup low-sodium soy sauce
3 tablespoons minced shallots
2 tablespoons dry white wine
2 tablespoons fresh lime juice
1 tablespoon minced fresh ginger
$1^1/2$ teaspoons brown sugar
2 garlic cloves, minced

Combine the peaches, plums, shallots, orange juice, parsley, lime zest, lime juice, jalapeño chile, mint, honey and ginger in a bowl and mix well. Chill, covered, until ready to serve. Trim the fat from the pork chops. Combine the soy sauce, shallots, wine, lime juice, ginger, brown sugar and garlic in a sealable plastic bag and mix well. Add the pork chops and seal the bag. Marinate in the refrigerator for 4 hours, turning the bag once or twice. Drain the pork chops, reserving the marinade. Preheat the grill. Place the pork chops on a grill rack coated with nonstick cooking spray. Grill for 7 minutes on each side or until cooked through, basting frequently with the reserved marinade. Serve the pork chops with the salsa.

Serves 4

BAKED CONCHIGLIE WITH SPICY PORK & SAUSAGE RAGU

2 tablespoons olive oil
6 ounces thinly sliced pancetta, chopped
2 pounds boneless pork country spare ribs
Salt and black pepper to taste
1 pound Italian hot sausages, casings removed
2 cups chopped onions
3/4 cup chopped carrots
3/4 cup chopped celery
6 large sprigs of fresh thyme
6 large garlic cloves, chopped
2 bay leaves
1/2 teaspoon dried crushed red pepper
2 cups dry red wine
1 (28-ounce) can plum tomatoes, chopped
1 1/4 pounds conchiglie pasta, cooked and drained
2 cups (8 ounces) packed coarsely shredded mozzarella cheese
3/4 cup (3 ounces) freshly grated Parmesan cheese

Preheat the oven to 275 degrees. Heat the olive oil in a Dutch oven over medium heat. Add the pancetta and sauté until brown. Remove the pancetta to a bowl using a slotted spoon. Season the pork with salt and pepper. Add 1/2 of the pork to the drippings in the Dutch oven and sauté for 7 minutes or until brown. Remove to the bowl with the pancetta. Repeat with the remaining pork. Add the sausages to the Dutch oven and sauté for 5 minutes or until brown and crumbly. Add the onions, carrots, celery, thyme, garlic, bay leaves and crushed red pepper. Reduce the heat to medium-low and sauté for 10 minutes or until the vegetables are tender. Add the wine and bring to a boil, stirring to deglaze the Dutch oven. Add the pancetta mixture and any accumulated juices and boil for 2 minutes. Add the undrained tomatoes and return to a simmer. Cover and bake for 2 hours or until the pork is tender. Remove from the oven. Uncover the Dutch oven and tilt to one side, skimming off the surface. Cut the pork into coarse strands, discarding the bones. Season with salt and pepper. (You may make up to 2 days ahead up to this point. Cool slightly and chill until cold. Cover and continue to refrigerate. Rewarm over low heat before continuing.)

Increase the oven temperature to 400 degrees. Stir the pasta into the pork mixture. Season with salt and pepper to taste. Spoon into a buttered 4-quart baking dish. Sprinkle with the mozzarella cheese and Parmesan cheese. Bake for 20 minutes or until golden brown.

Serves 8

CHICKEN IN THAI RED CURRY SAUCE

1/4 cup peanut oil or canola oil

2 to 3 tablespoons Thai red curry paste, or to taste

3 (13-ounce) cans coconut milk

1/2 cup chicken stock

1/4 cup Thai fish sauce

2 tablespoons brown sugar

8 Kaffir lime leaves (optional)

1 onion, cut into quarters lengthwise and sliced into 1/2-inch pieces

1 small can bamboos shoots, drained

1 red bell pepper, cut into bite-size pieces

8 ounces fresh green beans, trimmed and cut into 1-inch pieces

1/2 cup loosely packed fresh whole Thai or Italian basil leaves

4 boneless chicken breasts, cut into bite-size pieces

Hot cooked jasmine rice

Heat the peanut oil in a small stockpot over medium heat until hot but not smoking. Add the red curry paste and fry for 1 to 2 minutes, stirring constantly. Whisk in the coconut milk, chicken stock, fish sauce and brown sugar until thoroughly combined. Bring to a simmer, stirring constantly. Simmer for 10 minutes, stirring occasionally. Stir in the lime leaves, onion, bamboo shoots and bell pepper. Simmer for 10 to 15 minutes or until the bell pepper and onion are tender. Stir in the green beans and basil and simmer for 5 minutes. Add the chicken and bring to a low boil. Reduce the heat and simmer for 10 minutes or until the chicken is cooked through. Serve immediately with jasmine rice.

Note: Thai basil and Kaffir lime leaves can be found at the Thai stand in the Reading Terminal Market in Philadelphia.

Serves 4 to 6

LEMON SHERRY CHICKEN

3 chicken breasts, split, boned, skinned and pounded

1/2 cup (1 stick) butter

2 tablespoons sherry or vermouth

2 tablespoons fresh lemon juice

2 teaspoons grated lemon zest

1 cup heavy cream

Salt and pepper to taste

6 thin pats of butter

1 1/2 cups (6 ounces) freshly grated Parmesan cheese

Sauté the chicken in 1/2 cup butter in a skillet for 5 to 8 minutes or until cooked through. Remove to an ovenproof serving dish, reserving the drippings in the skillet. Add the sherry and lemon juice to the drippings. Add the lemon zest and cook for 1 minute, stirring constantly. Stir in the cream gradually. Season with salt and pepper. Preheat the broiler. Pour the sauce over the chicken. Place a pat of butter on each piece of chicken and sprinkle with Parmesan cheese. Broil until golden brown.

Serves 6

CHICKEN MEDITERRANEAN

For a wonderful addition to this recipe, serve over Broiled Polenta (page 137) as shown at right.

CHICKEN
2 garlic cloves, minced
3 tablespoons dry white wine
3 tablespoons olive oil
2 teaspoons finely chopped fresh marjoram
1 teaspoon salt
1 teaspoon freshly ground pepper
4 boneless skinless chicken breasts

MEDITERRANEAN SAUCE
1 tablespoon olive oil
2 tablespoons unsalted butter
4 whole artichoke hearts, cut into quarters
2 red bell peppers, roasted, peeled, seeded and cut into strips
1/2 cup white wine
1/2 cup chicken stock
2 tablespoons fresh lemon juice
2 teaspoons drained capers
10 Kalamata olives, pitted and sliced into quarters lengthwise
Salt and pepper to taste
1 tablespoon chopped fresh flat-leaf parsley

GARNISH
4 sprigs of fresh rosemary

For the chicken, mix the garlic, wine, olive oil, marjoram, salt and pepper in a bowl. Dip the chicken in the marinade to coat and place in a sealable plastic bag. Pour any remaining marinade into the bag and seal. Marinate in the refrigerator for 2 to 4 hours, turning occasionally to ensure even marinating. Preheat the grill. Drain the chicken, discarding any marinade and place on a grill rack. Grill for 5 to 7 minutes per side or until the juices run clear. Remove to a heated platter to keep warm.

For the sauce, heat the olive oil and butter in a large skillet over medium heat. Add the artichoke hearts and bell peppers and sauté for 5 minutes. Add the wine, chicken stock and lemon juice and bring to a medium simmer. Cook until the liquid is reduced by half and is of a sauce consistency, stirring occasionally to prevent burning. Remove from the heat to cool. Reheat the sauce and add the capers, olives, salt and pepper. Cook until heated through. Stir in the parsley just before serving.

To serve, place the chicken on individual serving plates and spoon the sauce over and around the chicken. Garnish each with a sprig of rosemary.

Serves 4

CHICKEN BREAST WITH PROSCIUTTO & FONTINA CHEESE

4 boneless chicken breasts
4 slices prosciutto
1/4 cup olive oil
2 tablespoons butter
1 garlic clove, minced
1 cup chopped fresh tomatoes
1/2 cup white wine

1/2 cup drained capers
1 teaspoon chopped Italian parsley
Salt and pepper to taste
1/2 cup (2 ounces) freshly grated
   Parmigiano-Reggiano
4 slices Italian fontina cheese

Preheat the oven to 375 degrees. Place the chicken between 2 pieces of plastic wrap and pound 1/2 inch thick. Lay 1 slice of prosciutto on each chicken breast and push into the chicken with the back of a knife. Heat the olive oil, butter and garlic in a large ovenproof skillet. Place the chicken breasts skin side down in the skillet and cook for 4 minutes. Turn the chicken and top with the tomatoes. Add the wine and capers and cook for 4 minutes. Sprinkle with the parsley, salt, pepper and Parmigiano-Reggiano cheese. Layer the fontina cheese over each chicken breast.

Place the skillet in the oven and bake until the cheese melts. Spoon the sauce over the chicken and serve.

Serves 4

ROSEMARY CHICKEN & ZUCCHINI SKEWERS

2 tablespoons grated lemon zest
1 1/2 tablespoons chopped fresh rosemary
1 tablespoon olive oil
1 teaspoon minced garlic
1 1/2 pounds boneless skinless chicken
   breasts, cut into 3/4-inch pieces
1 tablespoon olive oil

1 teaspoon minced garlic
2 tablespoons fresh lemon juice
1/4 teaspoon kosher salt
1/2 teaspoon pepper
1 1/2 pounds zucchini, cut into
   3/4-inch slices

Combine the lemon zest, rosemary, 1 tablespoon olive oil and 1 teaspoon garlic in a large sealable plastic bag and mix well. Add the chicken and seal the bag. Marinate in the refrigerator for 1 hour.

Preheat the grill. Whisk 1 tablespoon olive oil, 1 teaspoon garlic, the lemon juice, kosher salt and pepper in a bowl. Thread the chicken and zucchini alternately onto each of 12 skewers and place on a grill rack coated with nonstick cooking spray. Grill for 12 minutes or until the chicken is cooked through, turning once. Drizzle with the lemon juice mixture.

♡ For a more heart-healthy alternative, you may add additional vegetables, such as cherry tomatoes, red and green bell peppers and broccoli, and reduce the amount of chicken used per serving.

Serves 12

Asian-Spiced Chicken Thighs & Scallions

8 skinless chicken thighs, trimmed
2 tablespoons orange juice
$^3/_4$ cup dry vermouth
$^1/_3$ cup low-salt soy sauce
$^1/_4$ cup honey
2 tablespoons canola oil
2 large garlic cloves, minced
$^3/_4$ teaspoons ginger
$^1/_2$ teaspoon coarsely ground pepper
$^1/_4$ teaspoon ancho chile powder
8 scallions, trimmed
1 tablespoon canola oil

Cut 2 or 3 slashes $^1/_4$ inch deep in the skin side of the chicken thighs and place in a sealable plastic bag. Whisk the orange juice, vermouth, soy sauce, honey, 2 tablespoons canola oil, the garlic, ginger, pepper and ancho chile powder in a medium bowl until blended and pour over the chicken. Marinate in the refrigerator for 4 hours, turning several times to evenly coat.

Preheat the grill to medium heat. Coat the scallions with 1 tablespoon canola oil in a bowl. Drain the chicken, reserving the marinade. Place the chicken on a grill rack over the hottest part of the grill. Arrange the scallions around the chicken over the coolest part of the grill. Grill the scallions for 5 to 8 minutes or until tender, turning frequently. Remove to a heated platter and tent loosely to keep warm. Grill the chicken for 20 minutes or until cooked through. Remove to the heated platter and tent loosely to keep warm.

Bring the reserved marinade to a boil in a small saucepan over high heat. Cook for 10 to 15 minutes or until the liquid is reduced to $^1/_3$ cup and is of a syrupy glaze consistency. Drizzle over the chicken.

Serves 4

Pomegranate-Glazed Cornish Game Hens

Cornish Game Hens
3 Cornish game hens, cut into
  halves lengthwise
3 small onions, cut into halves
  lengthwise and cut crosswise into
  1/4-inch half-rings
6 sprigs of fresh parsley
6 sprigs of fresh mint
2 lemons, cut into slices 1/4 inch thick
24 baby carrots, peeled

1/2 teaspoon salt
1/4 cup pomegranate molasses
1/3 cup fresh orange juice
1 tablespoon olive oil
1 1/2 teaspoons salt
1/2 teaspoon hot Hungarian paprika, or
  1/4 teaspoon cayenne pepper
1/2 cup reduced-salt chicken broth

Pomegranate Sauce
3 tablespoons finely chopped shallots
1/4 cup dry white wine
3/4 cup reduced-salt chicken broth
1/2 cup pure pomegranate juice

1 1/2 teaspoons pomegranate molasses
1 1/2 teaspoons honey
1/2 teaspoon salt, or to taste
3 tablespoons unsalted butter

Garnishes
2 tablespoons chopped fresh chives

Sprigs of fresh mint

For the game hens, preheat the oven to 400 degrees. Rinse the hens and pat dry. Arrange the onions in 6 beds in a large shallow ovenproof pan. Place a sprig of parsley and a sprig of mint on each onion bed. Place 2 or 3 lemon slices on top of the herbs. Place 4 carrots crosswise over the lemon slices. Sprinkle 1/2 teaspoon salt over the cavity side of each hen half and place over the beds. Combine the molasses, orange juice, olive oil, 1 1/2 teaspoons salt and paprika in a bowl and mix well. Reserve some of the glaze for basting. Brush the remaining glaze over the hens. (You may make up to 8 hours ahead up to this point and store, covered, in the refrigerator. Remove from the refrigerator 30 minutes before baking to allow to come to room temperature.) Bake in the upper third of the oven for 10 minutes and baste with the remaining glaze. Add the chicken broth to the baking pan. Bake for 35 minutes or until the hens are brown and cooked through, basting with the pan juices every 7 minutes. Remove the hens to a heated platter and spoon some of the pan juices over the top. Reserve the unused pan juices and vegetables. Tent with foil to keep warm.

For the sauce, pour the remaining pan juices and vegetables in a strainer over a bowl, scraping up any brown bits. Reserve 1 cup of the pan juices. Bring the shallots and wine to a boil in a heavy saucepan. Cook until the liquid is reduced enough to just coat the shallots. Add 3/4 cups chicken broth, the pomegranate juice, pomegranate molasses and honey. Boil until the mixture is reduced by 1/2. Stir in the salt and remove from the heat. (The sauce may be made up to a day ahead up to this point and stored in the refrigerator.) Add the reserved strained pan juices to the sauce and bring to a boil. Boil until the sauce is thickened and reduced by 1/2. Whisk in the butter.

To serve, spoon the sauce over the hen halves and garnish with chives and sprigs of mint.

Note: Pomegranate molasses can be purchased at the Middle Eastern grocer at the Lancaster County Farmers Market.

Serves 6

Roasted Herb Turkey with Caramelized Onion & Balsamic Gravy 🏛

Turkey

6 tablespoons butter, softened
2 tablespoons chopped fresh thyme
2 tablespoons chopped fresh rosemary
Salt and pepper to taste
1 (22-pound) turkey
1 large onion, cut into quarters

1 cup low-salt chicken broth
1 bay leaf
2 large sprigs of fresh rosemary
2 large sprigs of fresh thyme
3 3/4 cups low-salt chicken broth

Caramelized Onion and Balsamic Gravy

1/2 cup (1 stick) butter
4 large onions, thinly sliced
1 1/2 tablespoons chopped fresh rosemary
1 1/2 tablespoons chopped fresh thyme

1 1/2 tablespoons all-purpose flour
1/2 cup balsamic vinegar
3 tablespoons honey
Salt and pepper to taste

For the turkey, mix the butter, chopped thyme, chopped rosemary, salt and pepper in a small bowl. Remove the turkey pieces from the turkey cavity and reserve. Rinse the turkey and pat dry with paper towels. Place on a rack in a large roasting pan and sprinkle inside and out with salt and pepper. Loosen the skin from the breast beginning at the neck and spread 1/4 cup of the herb butter between the skin and breast. Rub the remaining herb butter on the outside of the turkey. Place the reserved turkey pieces and onion quarters in the pan around the turkey. (You may make up to 1 day ahead up to this point and store, covered, in the refrigerator.)

Place the oven rack in the lowest position and preheat the oven to 350 degrees. (You may spoon your favorite stuffing into the turkey cavity at this point, if desired.) Tuck the turkey wings under and tie the legs together. Bake for 1 hour. Tent the turkey breasts and the tops of the drumsticks with foil and bake for 1 hour longer. Add 1 cup broth, the bay leaf, sprigs of rosemary and sprigs of thyme to the pan drippings. Continue to bake for 2 1/2 hours longer (3 hours longer if the turkey is stuffed) or until a meat thermometer inserted into the thickest portion registers 175 degrees, basting with 3/4 cup of the remaining broth and pan juices every 30 minutes to use all of the remaining broth. Remove the turkey to a serving platter and let stand for 30 minutes.

For the gravy, melt the butter in a large saucepan over medium-high heat. Add the onions and sauté for 40 minutes or until deep brown. Stir in the rosemary and thyme. Stir in the flour and cook for 1 minute, stirring constantly. Add the vinegar and honey and mix well. Simmer for 2 minutes or until thickened, stirring occasionally and adding the pan drippings from the turkey if needed for the desired consistency. (You may make the gravy up to 1 day ahead and store, covered, in the refrigerator. Reheat in the microwave or on the stovetop before serving.)

To serve, carve the turkey and serve with the gravy.

Variation:
For Traditional Gravy, strain the pan juices into an 8-cup measure and degrease. Heat 1 quart (4 cups) turkey gravy base in a saucepan over medium heat. Whisk in 3 tablespoons flour and the pan juices. Boil for 12 minutes or until the mixture is reduced to 7 cups, stirring occasionally. Season with salt and pepper. (Note: Turkey gravy base may be purchased at the Lancaster County Farmers Market.)

Serves 14

Grilled Achiote Turkey with Chile Gravy

Turkey
2 cups kosher salt
1/2 cup packed brown sugar
8 quarts cold water

I (12- to 14-pound) turkey
1/4 cup achiote paste
2 tablespoons vegetable oil

Chile Gravy
1/4 cup small dried red chiles, such as
   arbols, stems removed
1 1/2 tablespoons achiote paste
1/4 cup chicken broth
2 tablespoons vegetable oil
I white onion, chopped
I tablespoon coarsely chopped fresh mint

1 1/2 pounds ripe tomatoes, peeled, seeded
   and finely chopped
2 cups chicken broth
1/4 cup masa harina
1/4 cup chicken stock
Salt to taste

Garnishes
Chiles and sprigs of fresh mint

For the turkey, line a 5-gallon bucket with a lid with a large heavy-duty plastic bag. Dissolve the salt and brown sugar in the water in the prepared bucket. Rinse the turkey inside and out, reserving the pieces in the cavity for another purpose. Place the turkey in the brine mixture and cover with the lid. Soak in the refrigerator for 10 hours. Drain the turkey and pat dry inside and out. Fold the neck skin under the body and secure with a small skewer. Secure the wings to the body with small skewers if desired. Place the turkey on an oiled metal rack in a roasting pan that will fit inside a covered grill. Mix the achiote paste and vegetable oil in a small bowl and spread over the turkey. Loosely tie the drumsticks together with kitchen string. (The turkey may be made up to 1 day ahead at this point. Store, covered, in the refrigerator.) Preheat a gas grill to high heat. Place the turkey in the pan on the grill rack and cover the grill. Turn all of the gas settings to low. Grill for 3 hours or until a meat thermometer inserted into the fleshy part of an inner thigh registers 175 degrees, basting with the pan juices and rotating the pan 180 degrees every hour. Siphon off a generous 1/2 cup of the pan juices and reserve for the gravy. Remove the turkey to a heated serving platter, discarding the string and reserving the remaining pan juices. Cover loosely with foil and let stand for 20 minutes.

For the gravy, place the chiles in a small bowl and cover with very hot water. Soak for 30 minutes, stirring frequently to ensure even soaking. Drain the chiles, discarding the water. Process the chiles, achiote paste and 1/4 cup chicken broth in a small food processor or blender until smooth, scraping down the side to ensure an even purée. Spoon into a medium mesh strainer set over a bowl. Push the mixture through the strainer using the back of a spoon, being sure to scrape any paste off of the outside of the strainer. Heat the vegetable oil in a heavy medium saucepan over medium heat until hot. Add the onion and sauté for 5 minutes or until translucent. Add the achiote mixture, mint and tomatoes. Add 2 cups chicken broth and the reserved 1/2 cup turkey pan juices and mix well. Bring to a gentle simmer and partially cover. Continue to simmer for 30 minutes. Dissolve the masa harina in 1/4 cup chicken broth, whisking to break up any lumps. Strain the masa harina mixture into the broth, whisking constantly. Simmer for 10 minutes or until the gravy thickens enough to coat the back of a spoon, whisking constantly. Season with salt.

To serve, carve the turkey and arrange on a serving platter. Ladle the reserved remaining pan juices over the slices. Garnish with chiles and mint and serve with the gravy.

Serves 6 to 8

Turkey Black Bean Chili ♡ ⛭

1 tablespoon olive oil
2 cups finely chopped red bell peppers
1 cup chopped onion
1/2 cup finely chopped carrots
2 large garlic cloves, minced
4 teaspoons chili powder
2 teaspoons cumin

1 pound ground turkey breast
2 (15- to 16-ounce) cans black beans,
   rinsed and drained
3 cups canned low-salt chicken broth,
   fat skimmed from surface
1 tablespoon tomato paste
Salt and pepper to taste

Heat the olive oil in a heavy large saucepan or Dutch oven over medium-low heat. Add the bell peppers, onion, carrots and garlic and sauté for 12 minutes or until tender. Add the chili powder and cumin and stir to blend. Increase the heat to medium-high and add the turkey. Sauté for 3 minutes or until the turkey is crumbly and no longer pink. Add the black beans, chicken broth and tomato paste and bring to a boil. Reduce the heat and simmer for 1 hour or until the liquid thickens, stirring occasionally. Season with salt and pepper. Serve in miniature round bread loaves, if desired.

Note: You may make ahead and store in the freezer.

Serves 4

Coriander-Crusted Mahi-Mahi with Ginger Soy Sauce ♡

GINGER SOY SAUCE
1/2 cup reduced-sodium soy sauce
1/4 cup grated fresh ginger
1/4 cup fresh lime juice
1/4 cup chopped fresh cilantro
1/4 cup water
4 green onions, finely chopped

2 tablespoons rice vinegar
1 tablespoon dark brown sugar
1 teaspoon minced jalapeño chile
3/4 teaspoon minced garlic
1 teaspoon Oriental sesame oil

CORIANDER-CRUSTED MAHI-MAHI
4 (6-ounce) skinless mahi-mahi fillets
1/3 cup coriander seeds, crushed

Salt and pepper to taste
2 tablespoons canola oil

For the sauce, mix the soy sauce, ginger, lime juice, cilantro, water, green onions, rice vinegar, brown sugar, jalapeño chile, garlic and sesame oil in a medium bowl and let stand at room temperature for 1 hour.

For the fish, preheat the oven to 400 degrees. Press each fillet into the coriander seeds to coat and season with salt and pepper. Heat 1 tablespoon of the canola oil in a heavy skillet over high heat. Add the fillets and sear for 1 minute per side or until brown. Place in a large baking dish coated with the remaining 1 tablespoon canola oil. Spoon 1 tablespoon of the sauce over each fillet. Bake for 8 minutes or until the fish flakes easily. Heat the remaining sauce and serve on the side with the fish.

Serves 4

PAN-SEARED MONKFISH WITH HOISIN STIR-FRY & CITRUS NAGE

CITRUS NAGE

1 orange
1 lime
1 lemon

1 quart (4 cups) vegetable stock
2 tablespoons butter

FISH

4 (6-ounce) monkfish fillets
Salt and pepper to taste

Canola oil for searing
1 tablespoon butter

HOISIN STIR-FRY

1 tablespoon blended oil
12 (26- to 30-count) shrimp, peeled
   and deveined
2 heads baby bok choy
Pinch of salt

1 teaspoon light soy sauce
1/2 teaspoon mirin
1/2 tablespoon rice wine vinegar
1 tablespoon hoisin sauce

For the citrus nage, remove the zest from the orange, lime and lemon with a micro-plane zester and reserve. Peel the fruit and remove the sections from the pith. Combine the fruit sections and vegetable stock in a small saucepan. Bring to a simmer and cook until reduced by 1/2. Pour into a blender and add the butter. Process until emulsified and strain through a chinois or an extremely fine mesh sieve. Stir in the reserved zests to taste. (The zest is used to enhance the flavor of the nage with a sweet-and-sour effect, so add as much or as little as you like.)

For the fish, preheat the oven to 375 degrees. Season the fish with salt and pepper. Heat a cast-iron skillet to the smoking point and add the canola oil and fish. Sear the fish for 3 minutes or until light brown. Remove from the heat and add the butter to the skillet. Place in the oven and bake seared side down for 5 minutes or until the fish flakes easily.

For the stir-fry, heat a wok or sauté pan and add the blended oil. Add the shrimp to the hot oil and stir-fry until the shrimp turn pink. Add the bok choy and salt and stir-fry until the leaves begin to wilt. Deglaze the wok with the soy sauce, mirin and rice wine vinegar and cook until the liquid is reduced. Add the hoisin sauce and toss to coat.

To serve, place the stir-fry in the center of each serving plate and top with the fish. Finish the plate with the citrus nage.

Serves 4

Glazed Teriyaki Salmon

To really impress your guests, serve the salmon over Crispy Potato and Scallion Pancakes (page 129) with Red and White Pickled Onions (page 141).

1/3 cup orange juice	I teaspoon dry mustard
1/3 cup light soy sauce	I teaspoon lemon juice
1/4 cup dry white wine	Pinch of sugar
2 tablespoons vegetable oil	I garlic clove, minced
I tablespoon grated fresh ginger	2 (I-pound) salmon fillets

Combine the orange juice, soy sauce, wine, oil, ginger, dry mustard, lemon juice, sugar and garlic in a shallow dish or sealable plastic bag and mix well. Add the fish and cover the dish or seal the bag. Marinate in the refrigerator for I hour or longer.

Preheat the oven to 450 degrees. Drain the fish, reserving the marinade. Place the fish in a 9×13-inch baking dish and bake until the fish flakes easily. (You may also grill the fish.) Bring the reserved marinade to a boil in a small saucepan. Cook for 6 to 8 minutes or until the mixture is reduced by half, stirring frequently. Pour some of the heated marinade over the fish and serve the remaining marinade on the side.

♡ **For a heart-healthy alternative, serve the salmon over Braised Leeks (page 125).**

Serves 6

Pineapple-Marinated Salmon 🍳 ♡ 🎢

I (46-ounce) can unsweetened pineapple juice
1/4 cup light reduced-sodium soy sauce
2 (2 1/4-pound) center cut skinless salmon fillets,
   cut crosswise into 24 (1/2-inch-wide) slices
I tablespoon black sesame seeds

Bring the pineapple juice to a boil in a large saucepan over high heat. Reduce the heat to medium-low and cook for 20 minutes or until reduced to 3 cups. Pour into a bowl to cool. Stir in the soy sauce. Arrange the fish in a single layer in two 10×15-inch glass baking dishes. Pour the marinade over the fish, dividing evenly. Cover and marinate in the refrigerator for 3 hours.

Preheat the oven to 450 degrees. Spray 2 large rimmed baking sheets with nonstick cooking spray. Drain the fish, reserving the marinade. Place the fish flat side down on the prepared baking sheets. Bake for 4 minutes or until just cooked through. Carefully remove the fish with a spatula to a serving platter.

Simmer the reserved marinade in a medium saucepan over medium heat for 15 minutes or until reduced to I cup. Brush the fish with the sauce and sprinkle with the sesame seeds. (You may make I day ahead and store, covered, in the refrigerator. Let stand at room temperature for 30 minutes before serving.)

Serves 24

CRISPY THAI SNAPPER

THAI SAUCE

2 tablespoons fresh lemon juice
1/4 cup honey
1/4 cup soy sauce

2 teaspoons grated fresh ginger
1 teaspoon minced garlic
1/2 cup canola oil

FISH

1/2 cup whole grain mustard
2 eggs
2 tablespoons Dijon mustard
1 1/2 cups unbleached all-purpose flour
2 cups panko (Japanese bread crumbs)

4 red snapper fillets
1/4 teaspoon salt
1/4 teaspoon freshly ground pepper
1/4 cup (1/2 stick) unsalted butter

For the sauce, process the lemon juice, honey, soy sauce, ginger and garlic in a blender at low speed until smooth. Add the canola oil gradually, processing constantly until incorporated.

For the fish, whisk the whole grain mustard, eggs and Dijon mustard in a wide shallow bowl until well blended. Place the flour and panko separately in each of two 9-inch pie plates. Season 1 side of the fish with salt and pepper. Heat the butter in a large nonstick sauté pan over medium heat. Dredge the fish in the flour, shaking off any excess. Dip in the egg mixture to coat both sides. Dredge in the panko to coat, patting firmly to coat both sides well. Sauté the fish in the hot butter for 4 to 5 minutes or until the panko is golden brown. Turn the fish and sauté for 4 to 5 minutes or until the fish flakes easily.

To serve, reblend the sauce to ensure it is emulsified. Spoon a thin bed of the sauce on each heated serving plate and place the fish onto the sauce bed. Serve the remaining sauce on the side.

Note: You may need to finish baking the fish in the oven if the fish fillets are thick.

Serves 4

PAN-SEARED SWORDFISH WITH WARM TOMATO SALSA

1/3 cup dry white wine
2 teaspoons drained capers
1/8 teaspoon crushed red pepper
12 green olives, pitted and coarsely chopped
1/2 tablespoon chopped pimentos
2 garlic cloves, minced

1 (14-ounce) no-salt-added diced tomatoes
4 (6-ounce) swordfish steaks, about 1 1/2 inches thick
Freshly ground black pepper to taste
1 teaspoon olive oil
1 cup thinly sliced onion

Mix the wine, capers, red pepper, olives, pimentos, garlic and undrained tomatoes in a bowl. Sprinkle the fish with black pepper. Heat the olive oil in a nonstick skillet and add the fish. Cook for 4 minutes on each side or until the fish flakes easily. Remove the fish from the skillet and keep warm. Add the onion to the skillet and sauté for 4 minutes or until light brown. Add the tomato mixture and bring to a boil. Cover and reduce the heat. Return the fish to the skillet, soaking in the tomato mixture. Cover and simmer for 1 to 2 minutes or until the sauce thickens.

Serves 4

GRILLED SWORDFISH WITH SALSA FRESCA ♡

5 large ripe tomatoes, chopped
1 yellow onion, chopped
1/4 cup fresh cilantro, chopped
1/2 teaspoon salt
Juice of 1 lemon

1 teaspoon cumin
1 jalapeño chile, finely chopped
4 (6-ounce) swordfish fillets
1 tablespoon olive oil

Combine the tomatoes, onion, cilantro, salt, lemon juice, cumin and jalapeño chile in a bowl and mix well. Cover and chill for 24 hours. Let stand at room temperature for 1 hour before serving.

Preheat the grill. Lightly coat the fish with olive oil and place on a grill rack. Grill until the fish flakes easily. Remove the fish to a serving plate and top generously with the salsa.

Note: You may also bake the fish in a preheated 350-degree oven until the fish flakes easily.

Serves 4

LOBSTER TAILS MARINARA ALLA LAURA JEAN

3 large shallots, chopped
2 garlic cloves, chopped
1 handful fresh parsley, chopped
2 tablespoons extra-virgin olive oil
3/4 (15-ounce) can plum
  tomatoes, chopped with juice
Salt to taste
Cayenne pepper to taste

Dash of sugar
Paprika to taste
1 bay leaf
Chopped fresh basil to taste
Chopped fresh thyme to taste
Dash of oregano
1/2 to 3/4 cup sherry
5 lobster tails

Sauté the shallots, garlic and parsley in the olive oil in a large skillet until tender. Stir in the undrained tomatoes. Season with salt, cayenne pepper, sugar, paprika, bay leaf, basil, thyme and oregano. Stir in the sherry. Cover and cook for 30 minutes. Add the lobster tails and cook for 10 minutes longer or until the lobster meat is opaque. Remove the bay leaf before serving. Serve with your favorite vegetable or over hot cooked linguini.

Serves 5

FISH

Obtaining fresh fish is essential to preparing high quality food. If you shop at a place with a lot of traffic, you are guaranteed a high turnover, which almost always guarantees fresh fish. When you walk into a fish market, you should be greeted with the crisp clean scent of salt and ice. If you encounter a rank or vaguely foul smell, you should think about changing vendors.

If you are buying whole fish, look for moist skin, bright red gills, crystal clear eyes, and a fresh smell. If you prefer the convenience of buying fillets or steaks, be on the lookout for firm flesh, even coloring, and a moist appearance.

Mussels in Green Sauce

GREEN SAUCE
4 or 5 garlic cloves
$1/2$ cup packed fresh flat-leaf parsley
$1/4$ cup packed fresh cilantro leaves
6 to 8 green onions, trimmed
$1/3$ cup Spanish extra-virgin olive oil
2 tablespoons red wine vinegar
1 anchovy packed in oil
Pinch of crushed red pepper flakes
Salt and freshly ground black pepper to taste

MUSSELS
$1 1/2$ cups dry white wine
$1/2$ small yellow onion, minced
$1/2$ tablespoon cumin seeds, lightly toasted
2 pounds mussels, scrubbed and beards removed

For the sauce, pulse the garlic, parsley, cilantro and green onions in a food processor fitted with a metal blade until processed, scraping down the side of the bowl as necessary. Add the olive oil, vinegar, anchovy and crushed red pepper flakes and process to form a smooth paste. Season with salt and black pepper to taste. (You may make the sauce up to 8 hours ahead and store, covered, in the refrigerator.)

For the mussels, pour the wine into a medium saucepan. Add the onion and cumin seeds and bring to a simmer over medium-high heat. Add the mussels and return to a simmer. Cover and reduce the heat to low. Cook for 3 minutes or until the shells open. Drain in a colander, discarding any shells that do not open.

To serve, place the mussels in a large serving bowl. Add the green sauce and toss to thoroughly coat. Serve immediately with crusty French or Italian bread.

♡ To make heart healthy, reduce the olive oil in the Green Sauce to 2 tablespoons.

Variation:
For Shrimp in Green Sauce, substitute shrimp for the mussels. Cook the shrimp in the wine mixture for 3 to 4 minutes or until the shrimp turn pink and slightly curl. Serve tossed with the Green Sauce.

Serves 4

GRILLED SCALLOPS WITH WARM MUSHROOM VINAIGRETTE

WARM MUSHROOM VINAIGRETTE

1/2 cup balsamic vinegar
1/2 cup extra-virgin olive oil
1/4 cup Dijon mustard

Salt and freshly ground pepper to taste
1/4 cup blend of thinly sliced
   wild mushrooms

SCALLOPS

1 pound sea scallops
12 ounces mixed salad greens, including
   butter lettuce, arugula, water cress,
   radicchio and Belgian endive

I red bell pepper, seeded and thinly sliced
1/2 cup walnut halves, toasted

For the vinaigrette, whisk the vinegar, olive oil, Dijon mustard, salt and pepper in a small saucepan to blend. Add the mushrooms and bring to a simmer over medium-high heat. Simmer for 10 minutes or until the mushrooms are tender. Remove from the heat and cover with foil to keep warm.

For the scallops, preheat the grill to medium-high. Reserve some of the warm vinaigrette for brushing. Place the scallops on metal skewers and brush lightly with the reserved vinaigrette. Place on a grill rack and grill for 4 to 6 minutes or until the scallops are opaque, turning once. Cool slightly and remove from the skewers. Line a large serving platter with the mixed greens and arrange the bell pepper around the edge. Place the warm scallops in the center and drizzle with the remaining warm vinaigrette. Sprinkle with the walnut halves and serve immediately.

Serves 4 to 6

GRILLED SHRIMP WITH BLACK BEAN & MANGO SALSA ♡

3 cups canned black beans, rinsed and
   drained
1/2 teaspoon salt
2 garlic cloves, minced
2 mangoes, chopped
I red onion, chopped
I red bell pepper, chopped
2 tablespoons olive oil

1/2 cup fresh lime juice
1/2 cup chopped fresh parsley
I tablespoon cumin
I tablespoon chili powder
1 1/2 pounds large shrimp, peeled and
   deveined
Salt and pepper to taste

Mix the black beans, 1/2 teaspoon salt and the garlic in a bowl. Stir in the mangoes, onion and bell pepper. Whisk the olive oil, lime juice, parsley, cumin and chili powder in a bowl. Stir into the black bean mixture. Preheat the grill. Season the shrimp with salt and pepper to taste. Place on a grill rack and grill for 1 to 2 minutes per side or until the shrimp turn pink. To serve, spoon the salsa onto individual serving plates and top with the grilled shrimp.

Variation:
For Grilled Tuna with Black Bean and Mango Salsa, substitute tuna steaks for the shrimp and grill until the tuna flakes easily.

Serves 4

Mango Shrimp ♡ ⛲

4 pounds shelled small shrimp
6 ounces (³/4 cup) fresh lime juice
2 tomatoes, chopped
1 yellow onion, finely chopped
2 mangoes, cut into cubes
2 poblano chiles, seeded and minced

¹/2 cup chopped fresh cilantro
Dash of kosher salt, or to taste
2 avocados

GARNISH
Fresh cilantro leaves

Cook the shrimp in boiling water in a saucepan for 1 minute. Drain and cool. Combine the shrimp and lime juice in a glass bowl and marinate in the refrigerator for 3 hours. Add the tomatoes, onion, mangoes, poblano chiles, cilantro and kosher salt and marinate in the refrigerator for 1 hour. Peel the avocado and cut into cubes. Add to the shrimp mixture and toss gently just before serving. Garnish with cilantro leaves..

Note: You may substitute jalapeño chiles for the poblano chiles or mix the 2 together for a hotter spicier dish. If using jalapeño chiles, stir in just before serving to prevent the dish from becoming too spicy.

Serves 8 to 10

Tandoori-Spiced Shrimp

1 tablespoon cumin seeds
¹/2 cup plain whole milk yogurt
2 tablespoons finely grated fresh ginger
2 large garlic cloves, pressed
3 tablespoons fresh lemon juice
¹/2 teaspoon salt
Freshly ground pepper to taste

¹/2 teaspoon garam masala
4 drops of yellow food coloring
2 drops of red food coloring
24 jumbo shrimp, peeled and deveined
2 tablespoons vegetable oil
2 pounds fresh baby spinach
6 tablespoons unsalted butter

Place the cumin in a small dry heavy skillet. Cook over medium heat until the cumin darkens and becomes aromatic, stirring constantly. Remove from the heat to cool. Grind in a spice mill until finely ground. Whisk the yogurt in a bowl until smooth. Add the cumin, ginger, garlic, lemon juice, salt, pepper, garam masala and food coloring and mix well. Let stand for 15 minutes. Push the yogurt mixture through a sieve into a large bowl. Discard any solids. Stir in the shrimp. Marinate, covered, in the refrigerator for 1 hour.

Heat the oil in a stockpot over medium-high heat. Add a handful of the spinach and sauté until wilted. Repeat until all of the spinach is wilted. Continue to sauté until the excess moisture has evaporated. Cover and remove from the heat.

Melt the butter in a large nonstick frying pan over medium heat. Increase the heat to medium-high and add the undrained shrimp mixture. Cook for 3 to 4 minutes or until the shrimp turns pink and the sauce separates from the butter, thickens and clings to the shrimp. Do not overcook.

Place a small nest of the spinach on each serving plate using a slotted spoon or tongs, draining off any excess liquid. Divide the shrimp evenly on the nests of spinach and ladle the extra sauce over each serving.

Serves 8

BAHIAN SHRIMP STEW WITH SOUTH AMERICAN WHITE RICE

STEW
2 pounds uncooked shrimp, peeled and deveined
2 large garlic cloves
1 large onion, thinly sliced
2 tomatoes, peeled, seeded and chopped
3 serrano chiles, seeded and finely chopped
1/4 cup lemon juice
1 tablespoon chopped fresh cilantro
1 (13-ounce) can coconut milk
2 tablespoons dendê oil or fruity olive oil

SOUTH AMERICAN WHITE RICE
3 tablespoons vegetable oil
1 small onion, minced
1 green bell pepper, seeded and cut into quarters
1 garlic clove, minced
2 cups long grain white rice
3 1/4 cups boiling water
1 teaspoon salt

For the stew, place the shrimp in a glass bowl. Press the garlic over the shrimp and mix well. Let stand for 20 minutes. Combine the onion, tomatoes, serrano chiles, lemon juice, cilantro and 1/3 cup of the coconut milk in a saucepan and mix well. Cook over medium heat for 8 to 10 minutes or until the mixture is hot. Add the shrimp and dendê oil and simmer for 3 to 5 minutes. Stir in the remaining coconut milk. Bring to a simmer and remove from the heat.

For the rice, heat the oil in a saucepan with a tight-fitting lid over medium heat. Add the onion and sauté until translucent. Stir in the bell pepper and garlic. Add the rice and mix well. Increase the heat to medium-high. Cook for 2 to 3 minutes, stirring constantly to prevent browning. Stir in the boiling water and salt. Return to a boil and cover with the tight-fitting lid. Reduce the heat to low and cook for 20 to 25 minutes. Remove from the heat and let stand for 5 minutes. Remove and discard the bell pepper. Fluff the rice with a fork and serve with the hot stew.

Serves 6

Fettuccini alla Modense

6 tablespoons unsalted butter
$1/3$ cup frozen early peas
4 ounces fresh mushrooms, sliced
$1/2$ cup heavy cream
1 pound uncooked fettuccini
Salt to taste
8 ounces plum tomatoes, peeled, seeded and chopped
4 ounces prosciutto, cut into $1/4$-inch cubes
$1/2$ cup (2 ounces) grated Parmesan cheese
$1/4$ cup ($1/2$ stick) unsalted butter

Melt 6 tablespoons butter in a large sauté pan over medium-high heat. Add the peas and mushrooms and sauté for 3 minutes. Add the cream and continue to cook until the sauce is reduced by $1/4$.

Cook the pasta in boiling salted water in a stockpot until al dente and drain thoroughly. Add the tomatoes, prosciutto and cooked pasta to the sauce and toss to mix. Add the Parmesan cheese and $1/4$ cup butter and toss until the butter melts. Serve immediately.

Serves 6

Fettuccini Puttanesca ♡

2 (28-ounce) cans peeled Italian plum tomatoes, coarsely chopped
1 teaspoon chopped fresh oregano
$1/2$ teaspoon crushed red pepper, or to taste
$1/2$ cup kalamata olives, pitted and chopped
$1/4$ cup drained capers
4 garlic cloves, minced
4 anchovy fillets, chopped, or to taste
$1/2$ cup fresh Italian parsley, chopped
$1/4$ cup fresh basil, finely chopped
1 pound fettuccini, cooked and drained
Freshly grated Parmesan cheese

Bring the undrained tomatoes to a boil in a large sauté pan. Stir in the oregano, crushed red pepper, olives, capers, garlic, anchovies, parsley and basil. Simmer until thickened, stirring frequently. Spoon over the hot pasta and sprinkle with Parmesan cheese.

Note: To make this recipe even more heart healthy, use whole wheat pasta.

Serves 4

Basil & Arugula Pesto with Penne Rigate

Basil & Arugula Pesto

I package pre-washed baby arugula, or
  I bunch arugula, rinsed and trimmed

1/2 cup walnut pieces, or 2/3 cup walnut
  halves, toasted

1/4 cup extra-virgin olive oil

2 garlic cloves, pressed

1/4 teaspoon ground or freshly
  grated nutmeg

Salt and pepper to taste

I cup fresh basil leaves

1/4 cup extra-virgin olive oil

Pasta

I pound penne rigate

1/2 cup (2 ounces) grated Parmigiano-
  Reggiano

For the pesto, loosely pack the arugula in a food processor container. Add the walnut pieces, 1/4 cup olive oil, the garlic, nutmeg, salt and pepper. Set the lid in place and pulse to form a thick paste. Add any remaining arugula and the basil and pulse to form a thick paste. Heat the arugula paste with 1/4 cup olive oil in a skillet. Adjust the seasonings to taste.

For the pasta, cook the penne in boiling salted water in a stockpot for 9 to 10 minutes or until al dente. Remove the pesto from the heat and stir in the cheese. Stir in I to 2 tablespoons of the pasta water so the pesto is a consistency that is less than a paste but isn't runny. Place 1/2 of the pesto in a pasta bowl. Drain the pasta and add to the pesto. Toss for 2 to 3 minutes to coat. Add the remaining pesto and toss to evenly coat. Serve immediately.

Serves 4 to 6

Penne with Cannellini & Spinach

1/4 cup extra-virgin olive oil

2 large garlic cloves, minced

8 ounces chopped fresh spinach

I (14-ounce) can diced tomatoes

I (16-ounce) can cannellini,
  drained and rinsed

2/3 cup dry white wine

1/4 cup fresh basil, thinly sliced

Salt and pepper to taste

12 ounces penne, cooked and drained

Heat the olive oil in a large sauté pan over medium heat. Add the garlic and sauté for I minute. Add the spinach and sauté for 2 minutes or until wilted. Add the undrained tomatoes, beans and wine. Cook over medium heat for 5 to 7 minutes, stirring occasionally. Add the basil and simmer for I to 2 minutes. Season with salt and pepper. Add to the hot pasta in a serving bowl and toss to coat.

Note: To make this recipe more heart healthy, reduce the olive oil to I tablespoon and use whole wheat pasta.

Serves 4

Pasta with Pancetta & Chèvre

1 pound uncooked penne or ziti
1/4 cup olive oil
1 onion, chopped (about 2/3 cup)
4 ounces pancetta, chopped (about 1/2 cup)
3 tablespoons finely chopped fresh basil
1/4 cup oil-pack sun-dried tomatoes, chopped
1 1/2 cups chicken broth
4 ounces chèvre, crumbled into small pieces
Salt and pepper to taste

Garnish
Toasted slivered almonds

Cook the pasta using the package directions and drain. Heat the olive oil in a large sauté pan. Add the onion and sauté for 2 minutes. Add the pancetta and sauté for 2 to 3 minutes or until cooked through. Stir in the basil and sun-dried tomatoes. Add the chicken broth and cook for 5 to 7 minutes. Add the cooked pasta and chèvre and stir to mix. Cook over low heat for 1 minute. Season with salt and pepper. Garnish with toasted slivered almonds. Serve with a green salad and crusty French bread.

Serves 4

Fig & Prosciutto Sandwiches with Ricotta

10 slices crusty fresh bread
1 1/4 cups fresh ricotta cheese
4 teaspoons chopped fresh thyme
Salt and pepper to taste
10 slices prosciutto
10 fresh green figs or red figs, cut into wedges 1/4 inch thick
2 tablespoons honey, or more to taste

Spread each of the bread slices with the ricotta cheese and sprinkle with the thyme, salt and pepper. Place 1 slice of prosciutto on each bread slice. Arrange the figs on top of the prosciutto, dividing evenly among each sandwich. Drizzle the honey over the top of each. Serve sandwiches as open face.

Serves 5 to 10

Muffuletta Stuffed with Roasted Vegetables & Arugula Pesto

1 large round loaf of bread
6 large Portobello mushrooms, stems trimmed to 1/2 inch
Olive oil for brushing
Salt and freshly ground pepper to taste
1 large fennel bulb, thinly sliced
7 tomatoes, sliced
1 small red onion, thinly sliced and separated into rings
Basil and Arugula Pesto (page 175)
6 cups fresh basil leaves, rinsed
2 large yellow bell peppers, roasted, peeled and cut lengthwise into thick slices

Cut the bread horizontally into halves. Carve out the insides of the bread halves in whole pieces using a short serrated knife. Cut the insides of the bread into thin slices using a long serrated knife and cover. Pull out any remaining bread from the shells, leaving a 1/4-inch border. Cover the bread shells.

Preheat the grill to medium-high. Cut the mushrooms into thin slices and place on a grill rack. Brush with olive oil and sprinkle with salt and pepper. Grill for 2 to 3 minutes on each side or until tender. Brush the fennel with olive oil and sprinkle with salt and pepper. Grill for 3 to 4 minutes on each side or until tender.

To assemble the sandwich, cover the bottom bread shell with 1/2 of the tomatoes and 1/2 of the onion. Sprinkle with salt and pepper and drizzle with 3 tablespoons of the pesto. Cover with 1 cup of the basil and a layer of the sliced bread. Continue layering the second layer with 1/2 of the mushrooms, salt, pepper, 3 tablespoons of the pesto, 1 cup of the remaining basil and a layer of the sliced bread. Continue layering the third layer with the bell peppers, salt, pepper, 3 tablespoons of the pesto, 1 cup of the remaining basil and a layer of the sliced bread. Continue layering the fourth layer with the remaining mushrooms, salt, pepper, 3 tablespoons of the pesto, 1 cup of the remaining basil and a layer of the sliced bread. Continue layering the fifth layer with the fennel, salt, pepper, 3 tablespoons of the pesto, 1 cup of the remaining basil and a layer of the sliced bread. Continue layering the sixth layer with the remaining tomatoes, remaining onion, salt, pepper, 3 tablespoons of the pesto and the remaining 1 cup basil.

Replace the top bread shell on the bottom half, enclosing the vegetable layers and wrap in plastic wrap. Wrap some clean bricks in foil and place on top of the muffuletta to press down. Chill in the refrigerator for 3 hours or longer to press all of the air out of the sandwich so the layers will stay intact when served.

To serve, unwrap the muffuletta and cut into 8 wedges using a large serrated knife.

Serves 8

Desserts

Chocolate Bread Pudding ▥

I pound challah
$1/2$ cup light cream
$1/2$ cup heavy cream
I cup sugar
$1/8$ teaspoon salt
12 ounces high-quality semisweet or
  bittersweet chocolate, chopped

2 eggs
2 egg yolks
2 cups whole milk
I tablespoon vanilla extract

Cut the bread into $1/2$-inch slices and remove the crusts. Cut the bread into cubes. (You should have 6 to 7 cups of bread cubes.) Bring the light cream, heavy cream, sugar and salt to a boil in a saucepan, stirring constantly to prevent scorching. Remove from the heat and add the chocolate. Let stand for 2 minutes and whisk until smooth. Whisk the eggs and egg yolks in a large bowl until light. Whisk in the milk and vanilla. Add the chocolate mixture and whisk until smooth. Stir in the bread gently. Let stand for 1 to 2 hours, stirring occasionally and pressing the bread into the liquid to help absorb the liquid.

Preheat the oven to 325 degrees. Pour the bread mixture into a buttered shallow 2-quart baking dish, smoothing the top. Place on a rack in a larger baking pan. Add enough water to the larger pan to come $1/2$ way up the side of the baking dish. Bake for 55 to 65 minutes or until the center is firm when pressed. Cool for 45 minutes before serving. (You may make up to 3 days ahead and reheat by baking in a preheated 300-degree oven for 15 to 30 minutes or until a knife inserted in the center for 2 minutes comes out warm.)

Serves 8

Chocolate Decadence ▥

$1/2$ cup plus 3 tablespoons sugar
$1/4$ cup milk
2 tablespoons plus 2 teaspoons
  unsweetened baking cocoa
$1 1/2$ tablespoons butter
$1/2$ ounce unsweetened chocolate
5 tablespoons all-purpose flour

$1/2$ teaspoon vanilla extract
$1/8$ teaspoon salt
I egg white
8 teaspoons semisweet chocolate chips
Raspberries
Sweetened whipped cream

Preheat the oven to 350 degrees. Coat 4 muffin cups with nonstick cooking spray and sprinkle with 1 tablespoon of the sugar, shaking and turning to coat. Combine the remaining $1/2$ cup plus 2 tablespoons sugar, the milk and baking cocoa in a small saucepan and stir well with a whisk. Bring to a boil over medium heat and cook for 30 seconds or until the sugar dissolves, stirring constantly. Remove from the heat and stir in the butter and unsweetened chocolate until melted and smooth. Cool for 10 minutes. Whisk in the flour, vanilla, salt and egg white until blended. Spoon 2 tablespoons of the chocolate mixture into the prepared muffin cups. Sprinkle 2 teaspoons of the chocolate chips in each cup. Divide the remaining chocolate mixture evenly among each cup, spreading to cover the chocolate chips. (You may make 1 day ahead up to this point and store, covered, in the refrigerator.) Bake for 14 to 15 minutes or until set. Remove from the oven and cool for 10 minutes. Invert onto dessert plates and serve with raspberries and sweetened whipped cream.

Serves 4

MINTED CHOCOLATE MOUSSE

8 ounces high quality semi-sweet
   chocolate, melted
I ounce crème de mint
I ounce crème de cacao
4 cups (I quart) heavy cream

GARNISHES
2 ounces chocolate shavings
Chopped fresh mint leaves

Melt the chocolate in a saucepan over low heat. Remove from the heat and let stand for 10 minutes. Process the cooled chocolate, crème de mint, crème de cacao and cream in a blender until blended. Pour into individual parfait glasses and chill for 4 to 24 hours. (The mousse will thicken as it chills.) Garnish with chocolate shavings and chopped mint leaves just before serving.

Serves 6

DOUBLE CHOCOLATE SOUFFLÉS

2 tablespoons unsalted butter
2 tablespoons all-purpose flour
1/2 teaspoon instant coffee granules
   (optional)
I cup milk
10 ounces unsweetened chocolate,
   chopped
8 ounces bittersweet or semisweet
   chocolate, chopped

1/4 cup sugar
4 egg whites
1/4 teaspoon salt
2 tablespoons sugar
4 egg yolks
I cup heavy whipping cream
I tablespoon sugar
I tablespoon vanilla extract

Butter eight 3/4-cup ramekins and dust with sugar. Arrange on a rimmed baking sheet. Melt 2 tablespoons butter in a heavy saucepan over medium heat. Add the flour and coffee granules and cook for I minute or until bubbly, whisking constantly. Increase the heat to medium-high. Gradually whisk in the milk. Cook for 2 minutes or until the mixture thickens and boils, whisking constantly. Remove from the heat. Whisk in the unsweetened chocolate, bittersweet chocolate and 1/4 cup sugar until smooth. Pour into a large bowl and cool to room temperature, stirring occasionally.

Preheat the oven to 400 degrees. Beat the egg whites and salt in a medium mixing bowl until soft peaks form. Add 2 tablespoons sugar and beat until stiff and glossy. Whisk the egg yolks into the chocolate mixture. Fold in 1/4 of the beaten egg whites. Fold in the remaining egg whites 1/2 at a time. Divide the mixture among the prepared ramekins. (You may make the soufflés 2 days ahead up to this point and chill, or make a week ahead and freeze. Do not thaw the frozen soufflés before baking for 22 minutes.)

Bake for 17 minutes or until puffed and the center moves slightly when the baking sheet is shaken gently.

Beat the cream, I tablespoon sugar and the vanilla in a mixing bowl until stiff peaks form. Serve with the soufflés.

Serves 8

Bittersweet Chocolate Fondue with Pomegranate Syrup

Fondue

8 ounces high-quality semisweet
  chocolate, broken into pieces
1/2 cup heavy cream

3 tablespoons pomegranate syrup
1 teaspoon vanilla extract

Fondue Dipping Items

Fortune cookies
Pretzel sticks
Sliced apples
Sliced pears
Sliced kiwifruit
Orange sections

Pomegranate sections
Raspberries
Strawberries
Cubes of angel food cake
Cubes of pound cake

For the fondue, melt the chocolate in a double boiler over low heat. Whisk in the cream and pomegranate syrup. Heat until smooth and warm for serving. Stir in the vanilla. Pour into a fondue pot and keep warm over low heat.

To serve, spear your choice of the dipping items onto small forks or wooden picks and dip into the fondue.

Note: Use Chambord, Grand Marnier or Kahlúa instead of the pomegranate syrup for a variety of flavors.

Serves 4

Double Chocolate Espresso Tart

1/2 cup baking cocoa
1/2 cup (1 stick) unsalted butter
5 ounces good quality European dark chocolate
   (56 percent to 61 percent cocoa), coarsely chopped
1/4 cup instant espresso or coffee granules
1 1/2 cups granulated sugar
3 eggs
1/2 cup all-purpose flour
1/2 teaspoon baking soda
1/4 teaspoon salt
1 cup chopped macadamia nuts
Confectioners' sugar
Whipped cream
Bittersweet chocolate shavings

Preheat the oven to 350 degrees. Butter a 9-inch tart pan and lightly dust with some of the baking cocoa. Melt 1/2 cup butter in a double boiler. Add the remaining baking cocoa, the dark chocolate and espresso granules and heat until smooth, stirring constantly. Pour into a mixing bowl. Beat in the granulated sugar and eggs 1 at a time at low speed. Continue beating for 8 to 10 minutes.

Sift the flour, baking soda and salt into a bowl. Fold in the chocolate mixture and macadamia nuts. Pour into the prepared pan and bake for 25 minutes. Chill for at least 2 hours before serving.

To serve, cut the tart into wedges and sprinkle each wedge with confectioners' sugar. Top each with whipped cream and bittersweet chocolate shavings.

Serves 8

Lemon Tofu Cheesecake ♡ 🎀

Vanilla Wafer Crust
1 cup vanilla wafer crumbs
2 tablespoons pecans, finely chopped

2 tablespoons soy margarine, melted

Cheesecake
1 1/2 pounds silken tofu
16 ounces low-fat cream cheese, softened
3/4 cup sugar
1/4 cup all-purpose flour
1 tablespoon grated lemon zest

1 tablespoon vanilla extract
3 eggs
3 egg whites
Chopped pecans
Fresh fruit

For the crust, preheat the oven to 375 degrees. Combine the vanilla wafer crumbs, pecans and margarine in a bowl and mix well. Press in a 9-inch springform pan and bake for 8 minutes or until brown. Remove from the oven to cool. Maintain the oven temperature.

For the cheesecake, beat the tofu in a mixing bowl until smooth. Add the cream cheese, sugar, flour, lemon zest and vanilla and beat well. Beat in the eggs and egg whites 1 at a time. Pour into the cooled crust and bake for 50 to 60 minutes or until set. Cool to room temperature. Chill, covered, for 8 to 12 hours. Serve with chopped pecans and fresh fruit.

Serves 10 to 12

Pumpkin Cheesecake 👨‍🍳

Graham Cracker Crust
1 cup finely crushed graham crackers

1/2 cup (1 stick) butter, melted

Cheesecake
14 ounces cream cheese, softened
1 cup sugar
3 eggs
12 ounces pumpkin purée
1 tablespoon ground allspice

2 teaspoons ground cinnamon
1/4 teaspoon ground cloves
1/4 teaspoon ginger
Whipped cream

For the crust, mix the graham crackers with the butter in a bowl and press onto the bottom of a 10-inch springform pan.

For the cheesecake, preheat the oven to 300 degrees. Beat the cream cheese and sugar in a mixing bowl until soft and smooth. Add the eggs 1 at a time, beating well after each addition and scraping the side of the bowl. Add the pumpkin purée, allspice, cinnamon, cloves and ginger and beat until smooth. Pour into the graham cracker crust. Wrap the bottom of the pan in heavy-duty foil. Bake in a water bath for 35 minutes or until the cheesecake is set and lightly brown. Cool completely and serve with whipped cream.

Serves 12 to 14

SUMMERTIME PEACH COBBLER WITH ALMOND TOPPING

ALMOND TOPPING

I cup all-purpose flour
1/2 cup sugar
1 1/2 teaspoons baking powder

1/2 cup 2% milk
1/4 cup (1/2 stick) butter, softened
I tablespoon almond extract

COBBLER

1/4 cup packed light brown sugar
I tablespoon cornstarch
1/2 cold water
3 cups sliced peeled fresh peaches
1 1/2 cups blueberries
1 1/2 tablespoons butter

I tablespoon fresh lemon juice
1/2 teaspoon grated lemon zest
2 tablespoons granulated sugar
1/4 teaspoon ground cinnamon
Ice cream or frozen yogurt

For the topping, mix the flour, sugar and baking powder in a bowl. Add the milk, butter and almond extract all at once and stir until smooth.

For the cobbler, preheat the oven to 350 degrees. Combine the brown sugar and cornstarch in a medium saucepan and stir in the water. Add the peaches and blueberries and cook over medium heat for 15 minutes or until thick and bubbly. Add the butter, lemon juice and lemon zest and cook until the butter melts, stirring constantly. Pour into an ungreased 1 1/2-quart baking dish. Spoon the topping in mounds over the hot fruit mixture. Sprinkle with a mixture of 2 tablespoons granulated sugar and the cinnamon. Bake for 45 minutes or until bubbly. Serve warm with your favorite ice cream or frozen yogurt.

Serves 6

GINGERBREAD

5 cups all-purpose flour
2 teaspoons baking soda
2 teaspoons ground cinnamon
2 teaspoons ground ginger
I teaspoon ground cloves
1/2 teaspoon salt

2 cups molasses
2 cups hot water
I cup shortening
I cup sugar
2 eggs, beaten
Whipped cream

Preheat the oven to 350 degrees. Sift the flour, baking soda, cinnamon, ginger, cloves and salt together. Mix the molasses and hot water together in a bowl. Beat the shortening, sugar and eggs in a mixing bowl for 2 minutes or until creamy. Add the flour mixture and molasses mixture alternately, beating well after each addition. Pour into a greased 9×13-inch baking pan and bake for 45 minutes. Serve with whipped cream.

Serves 15

Balsamic Strawberries over Sweet Mascarpone Cheese

1/3 cup balsamic vinegar
2 teaspoons sugar
1/2 teaspoon fresh lemon juice
3 (1-pint) baskets strawberries, hulled
   and cut into halves
2 tablespoons sugar
1/2 cup chilled mascarpone cheese

1/2 cup chilled heavy whipping cream
1/2 teaspoon vanilla extract
2 tablespoons sugar

GARNISH
Sprigs of fresh mint

Combine the vinegar, 2 teaspoons sugar and lemon juice in a small heavy saucepan. Cook over medium heat until the sugar dissolves. Boil for 3 minutes or until the syrup is reduced to a scant 1/4 cup. Pour into a small bowl and cool completely. (You may make 2 days ahead up to this point and store, covered, in the refrigerator.)

Combine the strawberries and 2 tablespoons sugar in a large bowl and toss to coat. Drizzle with the balsamic syrup and toss to coat. Let stand for 30 minutes, stirring occasionally.

Whisk the mascarpone cheese, whipping cream, vanilla and 2 tablespoons sugar in a medium bowl until thick soft peaks form. Cover and chill for up to 4 hours.

To serve, spoon the mascarpone mixture into martini glasses or pretty goblets. Top with the balsamic strawberries. Garnish with sprigs of fresh mint.

Note: Balsamic Syrup can be purchased already prepared in certain grocery and gourmet food stores.

Serves 4 to 6

Summer Fruit with Wine & Mint

1 1/4 cups dry white wine
1/3 cup sugar
1/2 ripe cantaloupe, halved, seeded and cut into 3/4-inch cubes (about 3 cups)
1 (8-ounce) basket strawberries, cut into quarters
1 cup seedless green grapes, cut into halves lengthwise
1 tablespoon chopped fresh mint leaves

Bring the wine and sugar to a boil in a small saucepan, stirring until the sugar dissolves. Boil for 2 minutes and remove from the heat.

Combine the cantaloupe, strawberries, grapes and mint in a large bowl. Pour the wine mixture over the fruit and toss to coat. Cover and chill for 2 hours or longer, stirring occasionally. Spoon into a wide mouth jar with a tight-fitting lid and store in the refrigerator.

Note: For an elegant presentation, drizzle raspberry coulis or chocolate sauce on a flat plate and top with the fruit.

Serves 4

Banana Bundles with Chocolate Ganache

Banana Bundles
3/4 cup sugar
6 tablespoons unsalted butter
1/4 cup lime juice
6 bananas, cut into 3/4-inch slices
2 tablespoons Frangelico
1 (16-ounce) package phyllo dough
6 tablespoons butter, melted
1 tablespoon almonds, toasted and chopped

Chocolate Ganache
8 ounces semisweet chocolate
1 cup heavy cream

Garnish
Toasted almonds

For the banana bundles, combine the sugar, 6 tablespoons butter and lime juice in a skillet and cook over low heat until the sugar dissolves, stirring constantly. Increase the heat to high and cook for 5 minutes or until the butter melts and the mixture begins to brown around the edges, stirring constantly. Add the bananas and liqueur and cook for 2 minutes, stirring to coat. Spoon into a large bowl or on a baking sheet and let stand to cool.

Preheat the oven to 375 degrees. Carefully unfold the phyllo dough. Cut the dough into 6-inch squares and cover with a damp towel. Layer 3 sheets of the phyllo dough on a work surface, brushing each sheet with the melted butter. Spoon 1/6 of the banana mixture in the center and top with 1/6 of the toasted almonds. Bring the edges up and pinch the top to form a bundle. Repeat 5 times to form 6 bundles. Place the bundles on a baking sheet and bake for 10 minutes or until brown.

For the chocolate ganache, chop the chocolate and place in a bowl. Bring the cream to a boil in a saucepan. Remove from the heat and pour over the chocolate, whisking constantly until smooth.

To serve, place the banana bundles on a dessert plate and top with the chocolate ganache. Garnish with toasted almonds.

Serves 6

Ganache

Ganache is popular in the pastry kitchen. A French term referring to a smooth mixture of chopped chocolate and heavy cream, its origin dates back to the 1800s. The quality and taste of ganache depends on the quality of chocolate used. A chocolate with a velvety smooth texture will produce a ganache that is velvety smooth.

TIPSY PEARS

2 quarts (8 cups) apple cider
1 cinnamon stick
1/2 cup golden or dark rum
1/2 cup granulated sugar

1/2 cup firmly packed light brown sugar
8 ripe Bosc pears with stems
1/2 cup (1 stick) salted butter
Vanilla ice cream

Place the apple cider, cinnamon stick, rum, granulated sugar and brown sugar in a large stockpot. Bring to a slow simmer and simmer until the sugar dissolves, stirring constantly. Peel the pears and remove the cores from the bottom, leaving the stems intact. Place the pears in the cider mixture and bring to a simmer. Simmer gently for 15 to 20 minutes or until the pears are tender when pierced with a knife, turning carefully. Remove the stockpot from the heat and cool the pears in the cooking liquid, turning carefully several times.

Remove the pears to a bowl, leaving the cooking liquid in the stockpot. Remove the cinnamon stick and discard. Return the cooking liquid to a boil over medium-high heat. Cook until the liquid is syrupy and reduced to about 1 1/2 cups. Remove from the heat and add the butter, stirring until incorporated. Return the pears to the syrup and return to a simmer over medium heat, swirling the pears until heated through. Remove from the heat.

Place the pears upright on individual dessert plates with a scoop of vanilla ice cream. Ladle the syrup over the pears and ice cream and serve immediately.

Serves 8

PEAR SORBET ♡ 🎢

This recipe calls for Comice pears, but Bartlett pears are a good alternative in the winter and Taylor Gold pears (from New Zealand) are wonderful in the summer.

3/4 cup plus 1 tablespoon sugar
2/3 cup dry Alsatian-style white wine or
   dry Gewürztraminer
Seeds from 2 green cardamom pods
   (optional)

3 ripe Comice pears, approximately
   1 3/4 pounds
3 tablespoons lemon juice

Cook the sugar, wine and cardamom seeds in a small saucepan over medium heat until the sugar dissolves, stirring constantly. Increase the heat to medium-high and bring the syrup to a boil. Boil for 1 minute and remove from the heat to cool completely.

Peel, core and quarter the pears. Strain the cooled syrup through a fine mesh sieve into a bowl. Stir in the lemon juice. Process the pear quarters and strained syrup 1/2 at a time in a blender until smooth. Pour the puréed pears into a container. Cover and chill for 1 hour or longer, stirring once.

Pour the pear purée into an ice cream freezer container and freeze using the manufacturer's directions. The sorbet will be soft. For a firmer consistency, spoon the sorbet into a freezer container with a lid and freeze, covered, for 2 hours or up to 7 days.

Makes about 3 cups

FRUIT PIZZA

1 (20-ounce) package sugar cookie dough
16 ounces cream cheese, softened
1/3 cup sugar
1/2 teaspoon vanilla extract
Assorted fresh fruit such as sliced strawberries, sliced kiwifruit, blueberries,
  raspberries and mandarin oranges
1/2 cup peach or apricot preserves
2 tablespoons water

Freeze the cookie dough for 1 hour. Preheat the oven to 375 degrees. Line a cookie sheet with parchment paper.
Cut the cookie dough into slices and place close together to line the prepared pan. Bake for 12 minutes and
remove from the oven to cool. Invert onto a serving plate. Beat the cream cheese, sugar and vanilla in a mixing
bowl until smooth. Spread onto the cookie crust. Arrange the fruit decoratively on top. Mix the preserves and
water in a small bowl and brush over the fruit. (You may make 1 day ahead and store, covered, in the refrigerator.)

Serves 8

"Lemon Sticks" are a popular treat for children and adults alike at The Devon Horse Show and Country Fair.
An old-fashioned stick of lemon hard candy is inserted into a summer-ripe juicy lemon. The sugar from the lemon stick
"straw" sweetens the tart juice of the lemon, making for an irresistible combination.

Honey Apple Torte

^{1}/3 cup honey
2 tablespoons fresh lemon juice
3 Granny Smith apples, peeled and cut into 8 wedges each
1 cup all-purpose flour
1 teaspoon baking powder
^{1}/4 teaspoon salt
^{3}/4 cup granulated sugar
6 tablespoons butter, softened
^{1}/4 cup packed brown sugar
1 teaspoon vanilla extract
2 eggs
1 teaspoon grated lemon zest
1 tablespoon granulated sugar
^{1}/2 teaspoon ground cinnamon

Preheat the oven to 350 degrees. Bring the honey and lemon juice to a simmer in a large nonstick skillet over medium heat. Add the apples and cook for 14 minutes or until almost tender, stirring frequently. Remove from the heat.

Whisk the flour, baking powder and salt together. Beat ^{3}/4 cup granulated sugar, butter, brown sugar and vanilla at medium speed in a mixing bowl for 4 minutes. Add the eggs 1 at a time, beating well after each addition. Beat in the lemon zest. Add the flour mixture gradually, beating at low speed until blended. Pour into a 9-inch springform pan coated with nonstick cooking spray.

Remove the apples from the skillet with a slotted spoon, discarding any remaining liquid. Arrange the apple slices in a spoke-like fashion on top of the batter, pressing gently into the batter. Sprinkle a mixture of 1 tablespoon granulated sugar and the cinnamon evenly over the apples. Bake for 55 to 60 minutes or until the torte springs back when lightly touched in the center. Do not overbake. Cool in the pan on a wire rack. Cut into wedges using a serrated knife to serve.

Note: Serve the same day as prepared for the best flavor.

Serves 10

COOKING WITH APPLES

Use firm-fleshed varieties of apples such as Goldrush, Granny Smith, or Winesap as they will soften as they cook without falling apart. Choose apples that are firm with no soft spots, avoiding apples that are discolored, unless the variety is known for different markings. Always prepare apple dishes just before serving to minimize browning caused by oxidation. Protect cut apples from oxidation by dipping them into a solution of one part citrus juice and three parts water.

STRAWBERRY HAZELNUT TORTA

CRUST
3/4 cup whole hazelnuts with skins
3/4 cup sugar
I cup all-purpose flour
3/4 cup (1 1/2 sticks) salted butter, cut into pieces
I egg yolk
1/2 teaspoon vanilla extract

STRAWBERRY FILLING
I pint strawberries
1/2 cup sugar
I cup chilled heavy whipping cream
1/2 cup mascarpone cheese

ASSEMBLY
Small or quartered strawberries

For the crust, preheat the oven to 350 degrees. Pulse the hazelnuts in a food processor until finely chopped. Add the sugar and flour and pulse to combine. Add the butter and pulse until the mixture resembles coarse crumbs. Add the egg yolk and vanilla and process until the dough forms a ball. Flour your hands and press the dough in a 9-inch springform pan. (You must use a 9-inch pan or the crust will be too thick.) Gently make a depression in the center of the dough to form a 1/2-inch rim all the way around the edge. Bake for 45 to 50 minutes. Remove to a wire rack to cook completely. Loosen the crust from the side of the pan by sliding a knife around the edge. Remove the side of the pan. Slide a spatula under the crust to loosen it from the bottom of the pan.

For the filling, hull the strawberries and process in a food processor until puréed. Strain through a sieve into a liquid measure to yield I cup. Chill in the refrigerator. Combine the strawberry purée and sugar in a bowl and mix well. Chill in the refrigerator. Whip the cream in a mixing bowl until firm peaks form. Whisk 1/4 of the whipped cream into the mascarpone cheese. Fold in the remaining whipped cream. Gently fold in the chilled strawberry purée mixture. Chill for 4 to 24 hours. (The filling will become firm as it chills.)

To assemble, gently spoon the chilled strawberry filling into the torta shell. Sprinkle the top with small or quartered strawberries.

Variation:
For Chocolate Hazelnut Torta, melt 6 ounces high-quality bittersweet chocolate in a heavy saucepan over very low heat, stirring frequently. Remove from the heat and cool for 10 minutes, stirring occasionally. Whip 1 1/2 cups heavy whipping cream in a mixing bowl until stiff peaks form. Fold in 1/2 cup sugar, I tablespoon vanilla extract and 1/2 cup mascarpone cheese. Fold in the chocolate gently. Mound the chocolate filling into the prepared cooled crust and chill for 4 hours or longer. Garnish with whipped cream rosettes, chocolate shavings and toasted hazelnuts.

Serves 12

Tiramisu Eggnog Trifle

1 1/3 cups sugar
1/4 cup water
1/4 cup dark rum
3 tablespoons brandy
12 egg yolks
1/2 teaspoon grated nutmeg
32 ounces mascarpone cheese
2 cups whipping cream
2 teaspoons vanilla extract
1 tablespoon brandy

1 teaspoon dark rum
1 3/4 cups water
2 tablespoons sugar
6 1/2 teaspoons instant espresso powder
1/4 cup plus 3 tablespoons Kahlúa
2 packages ladyfingers
1 cup finely ground semisweet chocolate
   chips
Shaved chocolate curls or mascarpone
   cheese

Whisk 1 1/3 cups sugar, 1/4 cup water, 1/4 cup rum, 3 tablespoons brandy, the egg yolks and nutmeg in a metal bowl. Set the bowl over a saucepan of simmering water. Cook for 5 minutes or until thickened, whisking constantly. Remove the bowl from the heat and whisk in the mascarpone cheese 1/4 at a time until blended. Beat the whipping cream, vanilla, 1 tablespoon brandy and 1 teaspoon rum in a large mixing bowl until stiff peaks form. Fold in the mascarpone cheese mixture. Bring 1 3/4 cups water to a simmer in a saucepan and remove from the heat. Add 2 tablespoons sugar and the espresso powder and stir until dissolved. Stir in the Kahlúa.

Submerge each ladyfinger in the espresso mixture, turning to coat twice and shaking the excess liquid back into the pan. Place the dipped ladyfingers with the sugared side facing out around the bottom side of a trifle dish, pressing against the side of the dish. Layer the espresso ladyfingers, 2 cups of the mascarpone cheese mixture and 1/4 cup ground chocolate in the prepared trifle dish, making the chocolate layer visible through the side of the dish. Repeat the layers twice. Cover with the remaining espresso ladyfingers and add enough of the mascarpone cheese mixture to reach the top of the trifle dish. Sprinkle the remaining ground chocolate over the top. Cover and chill for 8 to 12 hours. Sprinkle with shaved chocolate curls or pipe mascarpone cheese decoratively around the top edge.

Serves 16 to 18

Frozen Lemon Trifle

A very refreshing dessert to serve on a hot summer evening.

1/3 cup butter
1/3 cup fresh lemon juice
2 teaspoons grated lemon zest
1 cup sugar
1/4 teaspoon salt

3 eggs, beaten
1 (2-pound) package pound cake
1/2 gallon vanilla ice cream, softened
Whipped cream (optional)

Melt the butter in a double boiler and stir in the lemon juice, lemon zest, sugar and salt. Blend in the beaten eggs. Cook over boiling water until thickened and smooth, stirring constantly. Remove from the heat to cool completely.

Trim the crust from the pound cake. Cut the pound cake into slices 1/2 inch thick. Layer the cake, ice cream and lemon sauce 1/2 at a time in a 2-quart glass dish, swirling the top. Freeze until firm. Remove from the freezer 30 minutes before serving and decorate with whipped cream.

Serves 8 to 10

Not Your Basic Chocolate Cake with Chocolate Truffle Frosting

CAKE
2 cups all-purpose flour
2 teaspoons baking powder
2 teaspoons baking soda
1 teaspoon salt
2 cups sugar
2 cups water
4 ounces imported unsweetened chocolate
6 tablespoons unsalted butter
1 teaspoon vanilla extract
2 eggs, lightly beaten

CHOCOLATE TRUFFLE FROSTING
$1^1/_3$ cups heavy cream
$1^1/_2$ cups sugar
6 ounces imported unsweetened chocolate, broken into pieces
10 tablespoons unsalted butter, cut into pieces
$1^1/_2$ teaspoons vanilla extract
Pinch of salt

For the cake, preheat the oven to 350 degrees. Butter and flour two 8-inch cake pans and line with waxed paper. Sift the flour, baking powder, baking soda and salt together. Bring the sugar and water to a boil in a saucepan over high heat. Boil until the sugar dissolves, stirring constantly. Pour into a bowl and add the chocolate and butter. Let stand until melted and slightly cool, stirring occasionally. Add the vanilla and mix well. Stir a small amount of the chocolate mixture into the beaten eggs. Beat the eggs into the chocolate mixture at medium speed until combined. Add the flour mixture all at once and beat at medium speed until smooth. Pour into the prepared pans and bake for 25 minutes or until the top springs back when lightly touched or a cake tester inserted in the center comes out clean. Cool in the pans for 25 minutes. Invert onto wire racks to cool completely.

For the frosting, bring the cream and sugar to a boil in a medium saucepan over medium-high heat. Reduce the heat to low and simmer for 5 minutes. Pour into a mixing bowl and add the chocolate, butter, vanilla and salt. Let stand until melted and mix until smooth. Set the bowl into a larger bowl of ice water for 40 minutes or until cool and thick, stirring occasionally. Beat or whisk until a spreadable consistency.

To assemble, spread the frosting between the layers and over the top and side of the cake.

Serves 12

WARM CHOCOLATE CAKES

1 cup sugar
2 tablespoons cornstarch
8 ounces bittersweet chocolate, chopped
1/2 cup (1 stick) butter, chopped

3 eggs
3 egg yolks
Whipped cream or vanilla ice cream

Preheat the oven to 350 degrees. Butter and flour two 3×5-inch loaf pans. Whisk the sugar and cornstarch in a large bowl to combine. Melt the chocolate and butter in a heavy medium saucepan over low heat, stirring constantly. Remove from the heat and cool for 10 minutes. Whisk in the sugar mixture until smooth. Whisk in the eggs 1 at a time. Whisk in the egg yolks. Spoon into the prepared pans. Bake for 22 to 25 minutes or until the cakes are puffed, dry, cracked on top and a cake tester inserted in the center comes out with some wet batter attached. Cool in the pans for 10 minutes. Invert onto 2 individual dessert plates. Serve warm with whipped cream or vanilla ice cream.

Variation:
For a special treat, serve the cakes with Kahlúa Whipped Cream (page 205).

Makes 2 loaves or 4 servings

CHOCOLATE CHIP VELVETY POUND CAKE

Great served for picnics or casual meals.

1 1/2 cups (3 sticks) unsalted butter
   softened
8 ounces cream cheese, softened
3 cups sugar
1 tablespoon vanilla extract

6 eggs, at room temperature
3 cups cake flour, sifted
2 cups miniature semisweet chocolate
   chips

Preheat the oven to 325 degrees. Lightly grease a 10-inch tube pan with butter or vegetable oil. Beat the butter, cream cheese, sugar and vanilla at medium-high speed in a medium mixing bowl for 2 minutes or until light and fluffy, stopping once or twice to scrape the bowl with a rubber spatula. Add the eggs 1 at a time, beating at medium speed for 10 seconds after each addition and scraping the bowl after each addition. Beat for 30 seconds longer. Stir the cake flour into the batter with a rubber spatula. Beat at low speed for 5 seconds, scraping the side of the bowl. Beat for 5 to 10 seconds longer or until the batter is smooth and even. Stir in the chocolate chips. Pour the batter into the prepared pan and bake on the center oven rack for 1 hour and 35 minutes or until golden brown and firm to the touch and a tester inserted in the center comes out clean. Remove from the oven and cool in the pan completely. Invert onto a cake plate and cut into slices to serve. You may drizzle the pound cake with Chocolate Ganache (page 187) if desired.

Variations:
For Vanilla Pound Cake, omit the chocolate chips.

For Almond Pound Cake, omit the chocolate chips and use 1 teaspoon almond extract and 2 teaspoons vanilla extract.

Serves 12 to 16

Peanut Butter Cupcakes with Milk Chocolate Candy Bar Frosting

CUPCAKES

2 cups all-purpose flour
1 1/2 teaspoons baking soda
3/4 teaspoon baking powder
1 teaspoon salt
2 cups sugar
2 tablespoons unsalted butter, softened

1/2 cup chunky peanut butter
2 eggs
1 cup sour cream
1 tablespoon vanilla extract
2/3 cup water

MILK CHOCOLATE CANDY BAR FROSTING

2/3 cup heavy cream
1/4 cup confectioners' sugar, sifted

1 pound high quality milk chocolate
   candy bars, broken into pieces

ASSEMBLY

Ice Cream

For the cupcakes, preheat the oven to 350 degrees. Line 24 muffin cups with paper liners. Sift the flour, baking soda, baking powder and salt together. Beat the sugar, butter and peanut butter in a large mixing bowl until light and fluffy. Add the eggs 1 at a time, beating well after each addition. Beat in the sour cream, vanilla and water. Add the flour mixture and beat for 2 minutes. Spoon the batter into the prepared muffin cups. Bake on the middle oven rack for 15 to 18 minutes or until a cake tester inserted in the center comes out clean. Cool in the pans on wire racks for 15 minutes. Remove from the pans to cool completely. (You may make the cupcakes 1 day in advance and wrap tightly. Store at room temperature.)

For the frosting, whisk the cream and confectioners' sugar in a double boiler over barely simmering water. Add the chocolate and cook until smooth, whisking occasionally. Remove from the heat, leaving the top of the double boiler set over the water.

To assemble, spread 2 tablespoons of the frosting over each cupcake. Serve with ice cream.

Serves 24

CHOCOLATE ALMOND BISCOTTI

2 cups all-purpose flour
1/2 cup imported unsweetened baking cocoa
1 teaspoon baking soda
1/4 teaspoon salt
6 tablespoons unsalted butter, softened
1 cup sugar
2 eggs
1 teaspoon vanilla extract
1 cup (6 ounces) chocolate chips
1 cup blanched almonds, lightly toasted

Preheat the oven to 350 degrees. Whisk the flour, baking cocoa, baking soda and salt together. Beat the butter and sugar in a mixing bowl until light and fluffy. Add the eggs and vanilla and beat well. Beat in the flour mixture. Stir in the chocolate chips and almonds.

Shape into a slightly flattened 4×12-inch log running from corner to corner on a baking sheet lined with Silpat. Bake for 25 minutes or until slightly firm. Cool on the baking sheet for 5 minutes.

Reduce the oven temperature to 300 degrees. Cut the log diagonally into 1-inch slices using a serrated knife. Place cut side down on a baking sheet lined with silpat. Bake for 8 minutes or until the biscotti is crisp on the outside and soft in the center. Remove from the oven and cool on the baking sheet.

Note: You may also use your favorite kind of nuts or dried fruit in this recipe. White chocolate chips may be used instead of chocolate chips.

Makes 1 dozen

COFFEE WITH DESSERT

Which coffee to serve with what dessert? Like wines, coffee can either complement a food or clash with it. The bright, snappy floral and "winey" flavors of East African coffees, such as the Kenyan and Ethiopian blends, or the light and fragrant beans from Mexico will go well with muffins and other rich breakfast foods. They also pair well with fruits and sorbets.

To accent the flavors of light desserts such as cakes, cookies, and fruit-filled pies, choose Guatemalan, Arabian Mocha, or Colombian coffee. Their added complexity, balance, and mild acidity really warms simple desserts. When serving something chocolate, think of rich, dark coffees such as espresso roast and Italian roast, which are perfect for your espresso machine. The more pungent French Roast is ideal when brewing by the pot.

Sinful Cocoa Brownies

Cocoa brownies have the softest center and the chewiest candy-like top "crust" of all because all of the fat in the recipe (except for a small amount of cocoa butter in the cocoa) is butter, and all of the sugar is granulated sugar rather than the finely milled sugar used in chocolate. Use high quality cocoa for these fabulous brownies.

10 tablespoons unsalted butter
1 1/4 cups sugar
3/4 cup plus 2 tablespoons unsweetened baking cocoa (natural or Dutch-process)
1/4 teaspoon salt
1/2 teaspoon vanilla extract
2 eggs, chilled
1/2 cup all-purpose flour
2/3 cup walnut or pecan pieces (optional)

Position the oven rack in the lower third of the oven and preheat the oven to 325 degrees. Line the bottom and sides of an 8×8-inch baking pan with parchment paper or foil, leaving an overhang on 2 opposite sides.

Combine the butter, sugar, baking cocoa and salt in a medium heatproof bowl and set in a wide skillet of barely simmering water. Heat until the butter is melted and the mixture is smooth and hot. Remove the bowl from the skillet and let stand until the mixture is warm.

Add the vanilla and stir with a wooden spoon. Add the eggs 1 at a time, stirring vigorously after each addition. Continue to stir until the batter looks thick, shiny and well blended. Stir in the flour. Beat vigorously with a wooden spoon for 40 strokes. Stir in the walnuts. Spread evenly in the prepared pan.

Bake for 20 to 25 minutes or until a wooden pick inserted in the center comes out slightly moist with batter. Remove the pan to a wire rack to cool completely. Lift up the ends of the parchment or foil liner and place on a cutting board. Cut the brownies into squares.

Note: Any unsweetened natural or Dutch-process baking cocoa works well in this recipe. Natural baking cocoa produces brownies with more flavor complexity and lots of tart, fruity notes. Dutch-process baking cocoa results in a darker brownie with a mellower, old-fashioned chocolate pudding flavor, pleasantly reminiscent of childhood.

Makes 16 large or 25 small squares

RITA'S WATER ICE

Think refreshing, mind-numbing cool. Think fresh, tongue-tingling fruit flavors. Think of a no-fat blizzard of a treat that is made with ice and real fresh fruit. Rita's Water Ice is much smoother than a snow cone and not nearly as slushy as a Slurpee®. The thirty different flavors, including strawberry, watermelon, blueberry, root beer, and the more traditional lemon and cherry, are made on-site in batches and served within thirty-six hours of making.

The history of water ice dates back to the days of ancient Rome when, in the summer, Emperors dispatched runners to the highest mountains to retrieve snow. For generations, the Romans, and then the Italians, enjoyed flavored ice. They ate it alone or mixed with ice cream to make gelati, a combination of Italian ice and soft ice cream. In the Italian neighborhoods of South Philadelphia, water ice has long been a summertime passion with small walk-up windows serving the young and old alike.

In 1984, Bob Tumolo, a former Philadelphia firefighter, opened his first water ice stand. Like his Roman ancestors, he mixed in real chunks of summertime fruit and called the business Rita's Water Ice. The ice was a big hit with Philadelphians, arguably the most discriminating flavored-ice eaters in the country.

Chocolate Chubbies

8 ounces semisweet chocolate
3 ounces unsweetened chocolate
1/2 cup (1 stick) unsalted butter
2/3 cup all-purpose flour
1/2 teaspoon baking powder
1/4 teaspoon salt
3 eggs, at room temperature

1 1/4 cups sugar
2 teaspoons vanilla extract
1 1/2 cups (9 ounces) semisweet
   chocolate chips
1 1/2 cups chopped toasted walnuts
1 1/2 cups chopped toasted pecans

Preheat the oven to 325 degrees. Melt the semisweet chocolate, unsweetened chocolate and butter in a double boiler over simmering water. Remove from the heat and cool to room temperature. Mix the flour, baking powder and salt together.

Beat the eggs and sugar in a mixing bowl until a ribbon forms when the beaters are lifted. Beat in the chocolate mixture and vanilla. Stir in the flour mixture until just combined. Do not overmix. Stir in the chocolate chips, walnuts and pecans.

Drop the dough by 1/4 cupfuls 2 inches apart onto 3 greased cookie sheets. Do not flatten. Bake for 10 to 12 minutes or until barely firm and the tops are just dry and slightly cracked. Cool on the cookie sheets for 2 minutes. Gently remove to wire racks to cool completely.

Makes 25

Jennifer's Jumbles

3/4 cup pecan halves
1 1/4 cups unblanched whole almonds
1 cup plus 2 tablespoons all-purpose
   bleached flour
1 teaspoon baking soda
1/4 teaspoon salt
1/2 cup (1 stick) unsalted butter, softened

1/2 cup granulated sugar
1/4 cup firmly packed light brown sugar
1 egg
3/4 teaspoon vanilla extract
1 cup (6 ounces) semisweet chocolate chips
1 1/2 cups raisins

Preheat the oven to 350 degrees. Place the pecan halves and almonds on a cookie sheet and bake for 7 minutes or until toasted, stirring occasionally. Cool completely and coarsely chop.

Sift the flour, baking soda and salt into a small bowl and whisk to mix evenly. Beat the butter, granulated sugar and brown sugar in a mixing bowl until light and fluffy. Beat in the egg and vanilla until blended. Beat in the flour mixture at low speed until incorporated.

Mix the chocolate chips, raisins, toasted pecans and toasted almonds in a large bowl. Add the batter and mix together evenly with a large spoon. Drop the cookies by soup spoonfuls onto cookie sheets and bake for 8 to 10 minutes or until just golden brown. (The cookies will flatten during baking.) Remove to wire racks to cool.

Makes 3 dozen

CARROT CAKE SANDWICH COOKIES

COOKIES
I cup plus 2 tablespoons all-purpose flour
I teaspoon ground cinnamon
$1/2$ teaspoon baking soda
$1/2$ teaspoon salt
$1/2$ cup (I stick) unsalted butter, softened
$1/3$ cup plus 2 tablespoons packed light brown sugar
$1/3$ cup plus 2 tablespoons granulated sugar
I egg
2 teaspoons vanilla extract
I cup grated carrots
I cup chopped walnuts
$1/2$ cup raisins

CINNAMON CREAM CHEESE FILLING
8 ounces cream cheese, softened
$1/4$ cup honey
I tablespoon vanilla extract
I teaspoon ground cinnamon

For the cookies, preheat the oven to 375 degrees. Whisk the flour, cinnamon, baking soda and salt in a bowl. Beat the butter, brown sugar, granulated sugar, egg and vanilla at medium speed for 7 minutes or until light and fluffy. Add the carrots, walnuts and raisins and beat at low speed to combine. Add the flour mixture and beat until just combined. Drop by $1/2$ tablespoonfuls on cookie sheets sprayed with nonstick cooking spray. Bake for 10 to 12 minutes or until golden brown, changing
the positions of the cookie sheets in the oven $1/2$ way through baking. Cool on the cookie sheets for I minute. Remove to wire racks to cool completely.

For the filling, beat the cream cheese, honey, vanilla and cinnamon in a mixing bowl until smooth.

To assemble, spread about I tablespoon of filling on the flat side of $1/2$ of the cookies. Place the flat side of the remaining cookies on top of the filling. Serve within 24 hours.

Makes 10 to 12 small sandwich cookies

GINGER CRACK COOKIES

2 cups all-purpose flour
1 3/4 teaspoons baking soda
1/4 teaspoon baking powder
1/2 teaspoon salt
2 1/4 teaspoons ground ginger
1 teaspoon ground cinnamon
3/4 teaspoon freshly grated nutmeg
1/4 teaspoon ground allspice
1/2 cup shortening
1/4 cup (1/2 stick) unsalted butter, softened
3/4 cup sugar
1 egg
1/4 cup plus 1 tablespoon mild unsulphured molasses
1 teaspoon vanilla extract
2/3 cup chopped crystallized ginger
1/2 cup clear medium-coarse decorator sugar for rolling

Sift the flour, baking soda, baking powder, salt, ground ginger, cinnamon, nutmeg and allspice together. Beat the shortening and butter in a mixing bowl until creamy. Add the sugar and beat for 1 minute. Beat in the egg, molasses and vanilla. Add the flour mixture 1/2 at a time, beating at low speed after each addition until the flour is absorbed. Stir in the crystallized ginger. (The dough will be stiff and sticky.) Flatten the dough and wrap in plastic wrap. Chill for 2 to 3 hours.

Preheat the oven to 375 degrees. Line large cookie sheets with parchment paper. Shape 1 tablespoon of dough at a time into a ball and roll in the decorator sugar. Place 3 inches apart on the prepared cookie sheets. Bake for 11 minutes or until the cookies puff up and flatten out. Cool on the cookie sheets for 1 minute. Remove to wire racks to cool completely.

Makes 2 dozen

Banana Cream Crunch Pie

Chocolate Crust

I package chocolate wafer cookies, crushed

³/4 cup (1¹/2 sticks) butter, melted

Pie

I (3-ounce) package banana cream instant pudding mix

I cup 2% milk or whole milk

¹/4 cup Kahlúa or other coffee-flavored liqueur

2 cups heavy whipping cream

I tablespoon vanilla extract

3 bananas, sliced

I tablespoon Kahlúa or other coffee-flavored liqueur

3 (I-ounce) bars toffee candy, such as Skor or Heath bars, chopped

Garnish

Sliced bananas

For the crust, preheat the oven to 350 degrees. Combine the cookie crumbs and butter in a bowl and mix well. Press in a glass pie plate. Bake for 8 to 10 minutes or until set. Remove from the oven to cool.

For the pie, whisk the pudding mix, milk and ¹/4 cup Kahlúa in a medium bowl until smooth. Beat the cream and vanilla in a mixing bowl until stiff peaks form. Fold I cup of the whipped cream into the pudding mixture. Store the remaining whipped cream in the refrigerator until ready to serve.

Toss the bananas with I tablespoon Kahlúa in a bowl. Arrange evenly in the cooled crust. Sprinkle ¹/2 of the chopped candy over the bananas. Spoon the pudding mixture over the candy. Cover and chill for 2 hours or until set.

To serve, spoon the remaining whipped cream on top of the pie and spread evenly. Garnish with sliced bananas and sprinkle with the remaining chopped candy.

Serves 6 to 8

TANGY BLUEBERRY TART

CRUST
3/4 cup (1 1/2 sticks) butter
2 tablespoons sugar
1 1/2 cups all-purpose flour

1 egg yolk
1/8 teaspoon salt

TART
1/2 cup sugar
1 cup crème fraîche
1/2 cup (1 stick) butter, melted
1 egg
2 1/2 tablespoons all-purpose flour
1 tablespoon buttermilk

1 tablespoon lemon juice
1 teaspoon grated lemon zest
1 teaspoon vanilla extract
1/4 teaspoon salt
2 cups fresh blueberries

GARNISH
Whipped Cream

For the crust, beat the butter and sugar at high speed in a mixing bowl for 1 to 2 minutes, scraping the bowl frequently. Add the flour, egg yolk and salt and beat until the mixture forms a ball. Wrap the ball in plastic wrap and chill for 1 to 2 hours.

Roll the dough into an 11-inch circle on a lightly floured surface. Place in a 9-inch tart pan with a removable bottom. Freeze for 1 hour. Preheat the oven to 350 degrees. Bake the frozen pastry for 20 to 23 minutes or until light brown. Cool on a wire rack.

For the tart, increase the oven temperature to 375 degrees. Process the sugar, crème fraîche, butter, egg, flour, buttermilk, lemon juice, lemon zest, vanilla and salt at high speed in a blender for 1 minute or until smooth. Reserve 1 tablespoon of the blueberries for the topping. Place the remaining blueberries in the cooled crust. Pour the filling over the blueberries. Bake for 55 to 65 minutes or until the filling is set. Remove to a wire rack to cool completely. Cover and chill until ready to serve.

To serve, garnish with whipped cream and the reserved blueberries.

Serves 12

CARAMEL ICE CREAM PIE WITH MOCHA FUDGE LAYERS

CRUST
1/3 cup chopped walnuts
2 tablespoons sugar
2/3 cup crushed vanilla wafers
    (about 32 cookies)

1/2 teaspoon ground cinnamon
2 tablespoons unsalted butter, melted

MOCHA FUDGE SAUCE
1 tablespoon instant espresso powder or
    instant coffee powder
3 tablespoons boiling water
1 cup sugar
2 tablespoons unsweetened baking cocoa
1 cup heavy cream

1/4 cup light corn syrup
4 ounces semisweet chocolate,
    finely chopped
2 tablespoons unsalted butter
1 teaspoon vanilla extract

ASSEMBLY
2 pints caramel ice cream
Whipped cream

For the crust, preheat the oven to 350 degrees. Process the walnuts and sugar in a food processor until finely ground. Add the crushed vanilla wafers and cinnamon and process to combine. Add the butter and process to form clumps. Press onto the bottom and up the side of a 9-inch pie plate. Bake for 10 minutes or until lightly toasted. Remove to a wire rack to cool.

For the sauce, dissolve the espresso powder in the boiling water in a small bowl. Mix the sugar and baking cocoa in a medium saucepan. Whisk in the cream, corn syrup and espresso mixture. Add the chocolate and butter and bring to a boil over high heat, stirring constantly. Reduce the heat and simmer for 4 minutes or until thickened, stirring occasionally. Remove from the heat and let stand to cool for 30 minutes. Stir in the vanilla.

To assemble, soften 1 pint of the ice cream at room temperature for 15 minutes. Spread evenly over the cooled crust. Coat the ice cream layer with 1/4 cup of the sauce. Freeze for 20 minutes or until the sauce sets. Soften the remaining ice cream. Spread evenly over the sauce layer. Coat the ice cream with 1/4 cup of the remaining sauce. Freeze for 4 hours or up to 5 days. (The remaining sauce may also be frozen and reheated just before serving.)

To serve, reheat the remaining sauce just before serving. Cut the pie into wedges and serve with whipped cream and drizzle with the remaining sauce.

Serves 8

Pumpkin Pie with Maple-Pecan Streusel

Maple-Pecan Streusel

1/3 cup chopped pecans
1/4 cup packed brown sugar

1 1/2 teaspoons maple syrup

Pie

1 refrigerator pie pastry
1 (15-ounce) can pumpkin
1 cup milk
1/2 cup packed brown sugar
1 tablespoon all-purpose flour
3 tablespoons maple syrup
2 tablespoons bourbon
1 teaspoon ground cinnamon

1/2 teaspoon salt
1 1/2 teaspoons vanilla extract
1/4 teaspoon freshly grated nutmeg
1/8 teaspoon ground cloves
1/8 teaspoon ground ginger
2 egg whites, lightly beaten
1 egg

Maple Whipped Cream

2 cups heavy whipping cream, chilled

2 tablespoons pure maple syrup

For the streusel, combine the pecans, brown sugar and maple syrup in a bowl and mix well.

For the pie, preheat the oven to 400 degrees. Fit the pie pastry into a greased pie plate, trimming and fluting the edge. Combine the pumpkin, milk, brown sugar, flour, maple syrup, bourbon, cinnamon, salt, vanilla, nutmeg, cloves, ginger, egg whites and egg in a large mixing bowl and mix well. Pour into the prepared pie plate and bake for 40 minutes. Gently spoon the streusel on the top of the hot pie to within 1 inch of the edge. Return to the oven and bake for 15 minutes longer. Remove from the oven and cool to room temperature.

For the whipped cream, beat the cream and maple syrup in a mixing bowl until stiff peaks form.

To serve, cut the pie into wedges and serve with the Maple Whipped Cream.

Variations:
This pie is also great served with Rum Whipped Cream or Kahlúa Whipped Cream.

For Rum Whipped Cream, beat 2 cups heavy whipping cream, 1/4 cup confectioners' sugar and 2 tablespoons dark rum in a mixing bowl until stiff peaks form.

For Kahlúa Whipped Cream, beat 2 cups heavy whipping cream, 2 tablespoons Kahlúa and 1 tablespoon granulated sugar in a mixing bowl until stiff peaks form.

Serves 6 to 8

IN-KIND DONORS

ADVANTAGE PRINT & DESIGN, Frazer, Pennsylvania

ANTHROPOLOGIE, Wayne, Pennsylvania

AUBUSSON HOME, Bryn Mawr, Pennsylvania

AVALON SEAFOOD, Avalon, New Jersey

BRUCE D. HORTON ANTIQUES, Stoudtsburg, Pennsylvania

CLAIR PRUETT STUDIOS, Strafford, Pennsylvania

FEASTIVITIES CATERERS, Berwyn, Pennsylvania

FLAG LADY GIFTS, Wayne, Pennsylvania

GATHERINGS FOOD SOURCE, Bryn Mawr, Pennsylvania

THE GARDEN SHOPPE, Strafford, Pennsylvania

HISTORICAL LOCATIONS MANAGEMENT, Radnor, Pennsylvania

HOME GROWN, Haverford, Pennsylvania

MARGARET KUO'S RESTAURANT, Wayne, Pennsylvania

SAVONA RESTAURANT, Gulph Mills, Pennsylvania

SCALLYWAG, Wayne, Pennsylvania

TERRA NOVA LANDSCAPING, Downingtown, Pennsylvania

TOTAL TABLE, Paoli, Pennsylvania

TWO PAPER DOLLS, Wayne, Pennsylvania

WATERLOO GARDENS, Exton, Pennsylvania

WHOLE FOODS OF DEVON, Devon, Pennsylvania

VIKING CULINARY ARTS CENTER, Bryn Mawr, Pennsylvania

ACKNOWLEDGMENT TO THE BOARD

The **Main Line Entertains** *Committee wishes to thank the Board for their support and assistance with the development of the cookbook.*

THE SATURDAY CLUB
BOARD OF DIRECTORS
2004–2006

Club President
Christine Kozeracki

Vice President for Community Outreach
Gail McCarthy

Vice President for Ways and Means
Mimi Killian

Vice President for Clubhouse Management
Anne Bolton

Vice President for Clubhouse Rentals
Marnie Bowen

Vice President for Membership
Molly Schneider

Vice President for Cookbook
Jennifer Newhall

Vice President for Communications
Jane Frantz

Vice President for Internal Affairs
Janet Heaton

Recording Secretary
Barbara Bashe

Treasurer
Marci Tierney

THE SATURDAY CLUB MEMBERSHIP
2004 – 2006

Dawn Altman

Ann Andrews

Anne Barker

Jennifer Bartos *

Barbara Bashe

Kirsten Bauer

Megan Belval *

Jessica Bemis

Colleen Bergan

Mary Kay Bergan

Mindy Jane Berman

Cindy Bevan-Wilson *

Julie Beverly *

Lesley Blatchford *

Jackie Blumberg

Anne Bolton *

Connie Bova

Marnie Bowen

Sandy Boyd *

Wendy Brooks *

Wendy Burchfield

Kathy Buttenbaum

Eileen Buys

Diana Calligan

Denise Campbell *

Sally Cantwell *

Julie Carbonell

Kristen Carroll

Stacy Clark

M. J. Chiles

Colleen Comerford *

Gayle Connelly

Louise Cook *

Kelly Cordray

Ann Corridan

Patellen Corr

Janie Craig

Ann Davies

Tina DeAngelis

Kit Dempsey

Denise Desatnick

Carol Devlin

Gail Dewey

Donna Dirks

Wendy Donaldson

Erin Downes

Beth Downey

Kay Dugery *

Stacy Enoch

Betty Ann Exler

Allison Ferlan

Teri Fischer

Nancy Fitzgerald

Jane Frantz *

Stephanie Frick

Lori Friel

Karen Galrao

Louise Games

Laura Gelrich

Rita Gosnear

Lynn Marie Gosnell

Terri Grabowski

Lisa Gresh

Gretchen Guttman

Anne Hain

Janet Heaton *

Nancy Hirschfeld

Diane Hoey

Priscilla Holmes *

Margaret Hondros *

Vaughn Honigman *

Bonnie Hoover

Lisa Horning *

Allyson Hotz *

Maureen Huffman *

Helene Jesnig

Jane Johnson

Peggy Julicher *

Mimi Killian

Christine Kozeracki *

Gretchen Larson

Carrie Lawlor

Leah LeComte

Patricia Leidy

Sara Leyden *

Sandy Lindberg

Pamela Lyons

Caroline Madden

Aileen Magee

Laura Manton

Laura Marino *

Kimberly Matranga *

Gail McCarthy

Colleen McCauley *

Amy McClatchy

Mary McKinney

Marlene Mentzer

Barbara Miller *

Alison Moore

Samantha Moran

Bonnie Motel

Lisa Mottes

Chris Nalbone *

Jennifer Newhall *

Trish O'Brien

Katie Opher

Jennifer Opie *

Tara Palmisano

Lynnsey Perrin-Hee

Leslie Peoples

Jennifer Peyser *

Colleen Philbin

Mary Ellen Pina

Lisa Powers

Kimberly Pratt

Nancy Rainer-Wallace *

Camille Richardson

Lisa Richey

Margaret Robertson

Michelle Robertson

Stacey Rohrbeck

Avis Rueger

Pam Ruggieri

Leanne Rush

Eve Sauter

Mary Kay Schenkel

Molly Schneider *

Kathy Sheward

Pam Shoenstein

Sandy Shusted

Tracy Sidoriak

Linda Sims

Donna Sinnott

Lisa Smith *

Theresa Smith

Jill Snyder

Rebecca Snyder

Kim Solari *

Suzanne Stohler

Katie Stratton

Peggy Sukonik

Nancy Sullivan *

Mary Liz Tadduni

Ann Taylor

Stephanie Thibault

Marci Tierney

Martha Thomson

Ali Trapp

Elissa Vogt

Kerry Walsh

Vicki Warner *

Maureen Weaver *

Susan Wiener

Kathy Wrabley

Suzanne Zelov

Liz Zubyk

* Denotes member of the Cookbook
Development Committee

209

RECIPE CONTRIBUTORS & TESTERS

Main Line Entertains *is a collection of the best 214 recipes selected from the many that were submitted. Our deepest gratitude to all of our family, friends, and members of The Saturday Club for sharing their treasured recipes; although we could not use all of them, each was unique and wonderful. To the recipe testers, we thank you for the extensive time required to test each recipe and for your invaluable feedback. We apologize to anyone whom we may have inadvertently failed to mention.*

Dawn Altman *
Ramaa Athreya
Linda Barnes
Barbara Bashe *
Elizabeth Beier *
Megan Belval
Colleen Bergan
Mindy Jane Berman
Mariann Bevan
Cindy Bevan-Wilson * +
Julie Beverly *
Judy Blatchford
Lesley Blatchford * +
Anne Bolton * +
Connie Bova
Marnie Bowen *
Eileen Buys
Tara Buzan
Terry Buzan
Diana Calligan
Denise Campbell *
Nancy Campolongo
Kristen Carroll
Michele Chupein
Mary Alice Clear
Teddi Cohen
Colleen Comerford *
Louise Cook *
Karen Dalby *
Karen Dalton * +
Tina DeAngelis

Anne de Cork
Maria Delany
Lou DePaul
Denise Desatnick *
Gail Dewey
Erin Downes
Kay Dugery *
Donna Eldridge
Leslie Flick
Jane Frantz * +
Suzanne Frensley
Sally Gale
Louise Games
Rita Gosnear
Courtney Gunsaelus
Anne Hain
Janet Heaton *
Trudy Herman
Nancy Hirschfeld
Priscilla Holmes *
Vaughn Honigman * +
Lisa Horning *
Allyson Hotz
Maureen Huffman
Valerie Jamison
Helene Jesnig *
Peggy Julicher
Susan Jurgensen
Cate Kelly
Carla Khabbaz
Mimi Killian * +

Jane Klotzbach
Christine Kozeracki *
Eileen Lambo
Gretchen Larsen
June Lehman
Sara Leyden
Sandy Lindberg
Cindy Lyons
Pam Lyons
Aileen Magee
Laura Marino
Barbis Marquardt
Kimberly Matranga * +
Judy Matusky
Neal McCarthy *
Linda Miller
Patricia Minogue Prestel
Constance Moore
Kathy Moore
Martha Moore
Elizabeth Mosier * +
Christine Nalbone * +
Jennifer Newhall *
Jennifer Opie *
Tara Palmisano *
Jennifer Peyser
Nancy Rainer-Wallace
Nancy E. Reinhard
Sharon Richardson
Michelle Roesler
Stacey Rohrbeck

Avis Rueger *
Leanne Rush *
Ira Saligman *
Molly Schneider *
Jim & Vicki Seidenberger
Bev Shapiro
Peggy Sheehy
Sandy Shusted *
Lisa Smith * +
Marcy Smith
Jane Spencer
Nancy Sullivan * +
Stephanie Swope
Mary Liz Doyle Tadduni
Marci Tierney *
Patricia Visich
Laura Vukovich
Vicki Warner * +
Maureen Weaver
Cortie & Janice Wetherill
Susan Wiener
Kathy Wrabley *
Pilar Yeakel *
Carla J. Zambelli
Suzanne Zelov *

* Denotes Recipe Tester
+Denotes Core Recipe Testing Committee

RESTAURANT & CATERER RECIPE CONTRIBUTORS

CLAY'S CREATIVE CORNER BAKERY, Berwyn, Pennsylvania

DILWORTHTOWN INN, West Chester, Pennsylvania

ELEGANCE BAKERY CAFÉ, Paoli, Pennsylvania

FACILE, Berwyn, Pennsylvania

FEASTIVITIES CATERED EVENTS, Berwyn, Pennsylvania

GEORGES' RESTAURANT, Wayne, Pennsylvania

GILMORE'S RESTAURANT, West Chester, Pennsylvania

JEAN GEORGES, New York, New York

333 BELROSE BAR & GRILL, Radnor, Pennsylvania

OLD GUARD HOUSE INN, Gladwyne, Pennsylvania

PEACHTREE AND WARD CATERING, Willow Grove, Pennsylvania

PLATE RESTAURANT, Ardmore, Pennsylvania

PROVENCE DISTINCTIVE CATERING, Trooper, Pennsylvania

SAVONA RESTAURANT, Gulph Mills, Pennsylvania

TASTE OF BRITAIN WITH EASY ELEGANCE, Devon, Pennsylvania

VIKING CULINARY ARTS CENTER, Bryn Mawr, Pennsylvania

WHERE THE MAIN LINE SHOPS
Photo Shoot Sponsor Credits

SPRING—ROUND-ROBIN TENNIS LUNCHEON FOR FOUR
Lifestyle Shot (page 18):
- *Simon Pearce crystal and pitcher, Mariposa china, Vietri china and accessories, Toll green tray, Grainware wine cooler/ice bucket, Hedges Artichoke Sphere, Neuwirth Cachepots, and New Growth English Garden Rose trellis provided by The Little House Shop.*
- *Grass place mats, green grass handbag, and flowered tennis racket cover provided by P. J. Hollyhocks.*
- *Yellow and white tablecloths, napkins, and tulle chair wraps provided by The Total Table.*
- *Floral arrangements, fabric bag for tennis rackets, and daisy tablecloth provided by Valley Forge Flowers.*
- *Wine provided by Sand Castle Winery.*
- *Location courtesy of a private residence, Villanova, Pennsylvania.*

SPRING—DEVON CARRIAGE MARATHON PICNIC FOR TWELVE
Lifestyle Shot (page 20):
- *Lemon sticks provided by the Devon Horse Show and Country Fair.*
- *Floral arrangements provided by Valley Forge Flowers.*
- *Children's clothing provided by Hartstrings Childrenswear.*
- *Women's clothing provided by Carol DeYoung.*
- *Location and the Main Line Express horses: Rosemont, Haverford, Strafford, and Radnor courtesy of Dr. and Mrs. Donald J. Rosato.*

Food Shot—Lemon Sticks (page 189):
- *Wire tray and lemons provided by Valley Forge Flowers.*
- *Produce and lemon candy sticks provided by Lancaster County Farmers Market.*

SPRING—WEDDING REHEARSAL DINNER FOR THIRTY AT ARDROSSAN
Lifestyle Shot (page 22):
- *Floral arrangements provided by Valley Forge Flowers.*
- *Wine provided by Sand Castle Winery.*
- *Location courtesy of Ardrossan, Villanova, Pennsylvania.*

SUMMER—SEASHORE, SEASHELL, SEAFOOD AVALON FOR TWELVE
Lifestyle Shot (pages 24 and 65):
- *Viking Grill, 53" wide with 3 grill areas and double side burners, model #VGBQ532-3RT in stainless steel, installed in stainless steel cart, model #BQC530T-SS, provided by Carl Schaedel and Co., Inc.*
- *Parrot stand provided by Weichert Realtors, Hoey Group, Avalon, New Jersey.*
- *Seafood provided by The Avalon Seafood Company.*
- *Linens provided by The Total Table.*
- *Tables provided by Main Line Rental.*
- *Table accessories provided by Anthropologie.*
- *Wine provided by Sand Castle Winery.*
- *Location courtesy of Mr. and Mrs. Donald Sheehy, Avalon, New Jersey.*

SUMMER—SUMMER COCKTAILS AT CHANTICLEER FOR TWENTY
Lifestyle Shot (page 26):
- *Black serving platters provided by Viking Culinary Arts Center.*
- *Bento boxes and fortune cookies provided by Margaret Kuo's Restaurant.*
- *Floral arrangements and orchids provided by Valley Forge Flowers.*
- *Location courtesy of Chanticleer, Wayne, Pennsylvania.*

Food Shot—Seared Spice-Encrusted Tuna with Pineapple Peppercorn Salsa on Chive Rice Patty (page 59):
- *Plates, placemat, chopsticks, and candle pagoda provided by Home Grown.*

Food Shot—Bittersweet Chocolate Fondue (page 178):
- *Martini glasses provided by Home Grown.*
- *Bento boxes and fortune cookies provided by Margaret Kuo's Restaurant.*
- *Floral arrangements, orchids, and lemongrass provided by Valley Forge Flowers.*

SUMMER—FOURTH OF JULY FAMILY PICNIC FOR EIGHT
Lifestyle Shot (page 28):
- *Antique library/dining table and floral arrangements provided by Valley Forge Flowers.*
- *White enamelware dinner plates provided by The Little House Shop.*
- *Wine provided by Sand Castle Winery.*
- *Water ice and accessories provided by Rita's Water Ice.*
- *BMW motorcycle and VW Toureg provided by Devon Hill BMW.*
- *Location courtesy of the Valley Forge National Historical Park, Valley Forge, Pennsylvania.*

Food Shot—Chilied Flank Steak and Tequila Fire Shrimp (page 146):
- *Cutting board and serving utensil provided by Viking Culinary Arts Center.*

Food Shot—Lemons with Water Ice and Sinful Cocoa Brownies (page 198):
- *Lemon water ice provided by Rita's Water Ice.*

FALL—BROOKE FARM FALL FESTIVAL
Lifestyle Shot (page 30):
- *Bench, urn, wire basket, and all floral arrangements provided by Valley Forge Flowers.*
- *Decorative three-tiered tray provided by P. J. Hollyhocks.*
- *Pedestal tray provided by Waterloo Gardens.*
- *Potted tree provided by Terranova Landscaping.*
- *Pumpkins, hay bales, and cornstalks provided by The Garden Shoppe.*
- *Costumes provided by Heirloom Designs.*
- *Decorative pumpkins provided by The Flag Lady.*
- *Location courtesy of B. J. and Richard Johnson, St. David's, Pennsylvania.*

Food Shot—Curried Pumpkin and Sweet Potato Soup (page 102):
- *Silverware provided by The Little House Shop.*
- *Floral arrangements provided by Valley Forge Flowers.*

FALL—RADNOR HUNT THREE-DAY EVENT BLUE RIBBON TAILGATE FOR TEN
Lifestyle Shot (page 32):
- *Table, chairs and bench set, candelabra, floral arrangements, and hat provided by Valley Forge Flowers.*
- *Tablecloth provided by P. J. Hollyhocks.*
- *Wine provided by Sand Castle Winery.*
- *Location courtesy of a private residence, Villanova, Pennsylvania.*

FALL—THANKSGIVING DINNER FOR TWELVE
Lifestyle Shot (page 34):
- *Lynn Chase (Winter Game Bird) china provided by The Little House Shop.*
- *Bountiful hydrangea and pomegranate table runner provided by Valley Forge Flowers.*
- *Wine provided by Sand Castle Winery.*
- *Waterford candelabra provided by Walter J. Cook Jewelers.*
- *Waterford crystal (Pallas) provided by Walter J. Cook Jewelers and Historical Locations Management.*
- *Location, antique ancestral sterling flatware, and chargers provided by Mr. and Mrs. Cortright Wetherill, Jr., Wide Rill Farm, Malvern, Pennsylvania.*

Food Shot—Winter Game Bird China Place Setting with Arugula and Leafy Greens Topped with Parmesan Bow Ties and Balsamic Apple Vinaigrette (page 98):
- *Lynn Chase (Winter Game Bird) china place setting provided by The Little House Shop.*
- *Emerald and diamond tennis bracelet, candelabra, and Waterford crystal provided by Walter J. Cook Jewelers.*
- *Floral arrangement and dog knife rest provided by Valley Forge Flowers.*
- *Table linens provided by The Total Table.*

WINTER—WINTER BRUNCH IN THE KITCHEN FOR EIGHT
Lifestyle Shot (page 36):
- *Decorating services, china, and accessories provided by Environments HC.*
- *Tortoiseshell serving utensils, wooden bowls, Onyx napkin rings, and handmade wooden fruit bowl provided by Home Grown.*
- *Floral arrangements provided by Valley Forge Flowers.*
- *Decorative pillows for the banquette provided by Scallywag.*
- *Vintage silverware settings circa 1825 provided by private owner.*
- *Kitchen design by Coventry Kitchens.*
- *Location courtesy of a private residence, Villanova, Pennsylvania.*

WINTER—ELEGANT DINNER PARTY FOR EIGHT
Cover and Lifestyle Shot (page 38):
- *Floral arrangements provided by Valley Forge Flowers.*
- *Location and wine glasses courtesy of Mr. and Mrs. Cortright Wetherill, Jr., Wide Rill Farm, Malvern, Pennsylvania.*

WINTER—HOLIDAY OPEN HOUSE FOR FORTY
Lifestyle Shot (page 40):
- *Decorating services, Ajka crystal, and vintage glassware and accessories provided by Environments HC.*
- *Magnolia leaf and berry garland provided by Valley Forge Flowers.*
- *Waterford candelabra provided by Walter J. Cook Jewelers.*
- *Fabrics for table linens provided by Aubusson Home.*
- *Vintage 1920s three-tiered brass bar cart provided by private owner.*
- *Crystal punch bowl provided by Bruce D. Horton Antiques.*
- *Gold serving tray, gold glass place mat, and gold bowls provided by Home Grown.*
- *Location courtesy of a private residence, Villanova, Pennsylvania.*

Food Shot—Fingerling Potatoes with Caviar (page 68):
- *China provided by Home Grown.*

ARDMORE FARMERS MARKET, ARDMORE, PENNSYLVANIA (page 50)
- *Location courtesy of Ardmore Farmers Market, Ardmore, Pennsylvania.*

LANCASTER COUNTY FARMERS MARKET, STRAFFORD, PENNSYLVANIA (page 51)
- *Photography Sponsors: Good Harvest Farm, D'Innocenzo's Bakery and S. Clyde Weaver.*
- *Location courtesy of Lancaster County Farmers Market, Strafford, Pennsylvania.*

The Braemore Toile fabric used in the design of Main Line Entertains *is available for purchase in fine fabric stores such as Calico Corners.*

* All other home accents were generously provided by Saturday Club members, friends, and homeowners of the Main Line.

INDEX

219

Main Line Entertains

THE SATURDAY CLUB

117 West Wayne Avenue • Wayne, Pennsylvania 19087

610-688-9746

Name _____

Address _____

City _____ State _____ Zip _____

Telephone _____ E-mail _____

Please send me _____ copies of *Main Line Entertains* at $29.95 each $ _____

Pennsylvania residents add 6% sales tax $ _____

Postage and handling @ $4.50 for first book,
$1.75 for each additional book $ _____

TOTAL $ _____

Method of Payment: [   ] MasterCard   [   ] VISA
[   ] Check or money order payable to The Saturday Club

Account Number _____ Expiration Date _____

Signature _____

Please allow three to four weeks for delivery.

Thank you for your purchase. All proceeds from the sales of *Main Line Entertains* support The Saturday Club's continuing efforts to fund charitable organizations throughout the Philadelphia area.

Photocopies will be accepted.